A Gift for: _____

Not one of all the good promises the
LORD your God gave you has failed. Every
promise has been fulfilled.
Joshua 23:14

From: _____

Joy for a Woman's Soul: Promises to Refresh the Spirit
Copyright © 1998 by Zondervan

Requests for information should be addressed to:

Zondervan, *Grand Rapids, Michigan* 49530

ISBN-10: 0-310-81011-6
ISBN-13: 978-0-310-81011-7

Excerpts taken from:

Because He Lives by Gloria Gaither. Copyright © 1997 by Gloria Gaither. Published by Zondervan Publishing House, a division of HarperCollins Publishers. All rights reserved.

Boomerang Joy by Barbara Johnson. Copyright © 1998 by Barbara Johnson. Published by Zondervan Publishing House, a division of HarperCollins Publishers. All rights reserved.

Bring Back the Joy by Sheila Walsh. Copyright © 1998 by Sheila Walsh. Published by Zondervan Publishing House, a division of HarperCollins Publishers. All rights reserved.

Friends Through Thick & Thin by Gloria Gaither, Sue Buchanan, Peggy Benson, and Joy MacKenzie. Copyright © 1998 by Gloria Gaither, Sue Buchanan, Peggy Benson, Joy MacKenzie. Published by Zondervan Publishing House, a division of HarperCollins Publishers. All rights reserved.

Joy Breaks by Patsy Clairmont, Barbara Johnson, Marilyn Meberg, and Luci Swindoll. Copyright © 1997 by Zondervan Publishing House, a division of HarperCollins Publishers. All rights reserved.

My Life Is in Your Hands by Kathy Troccoli. Copyright © 1997 by Kathy Troccoli. Published by Zondervan Publishing House, a division of HarperCollins Publishers. All rights reserved.

We Brake for Joy! by Patsy Clairmont, Barbara Johnson, Marilyn Meberg, Luci Swindoll, Sheila Walsh, and Thelma Wells. Copyright © 1998 by Patsy Clairmont, Barbara Johnson, Marilyn Meberg, Luci Swindoll, Sheila Walsh, Thelma Wells. Published by Zondervan Publishing House, a division of HarperCollins Publishers. All rights reserved.

All Scripture quotations, unless otherwise indicated, are taken from the *Holy Bible: New International Version*® . NIV®. Copyright © 1973, 1978, 1984 by International Bible Society. Used by permission of Zondervan. All rights reserved.

Scripture quotations marked NASB are from the *New American Standard Bible*, Copyright © 1960,1962, 1963, 1968, 1971, 1972, 1973, 1975, 1977 by the Lockman Foundation. Used by permission.

Interior design by Kris Perpich

Printed in China

09 10 11 12 /TSC/ 23 22 21 20 19 18 17 16 15 14 13 12 11 10 9

Joy
for a
Woman's Soul
Promises to Refresh
the Spirit

Table of Contents

Part III: Give Joy a Boost

Part IV: Share the Joy

Discovering
Joy

The Joy of Being Me

As I travel across the country to various speaking engagements, I meet concealed hurt, disguised hurt, disjointed hurt. Pain is a normal part of life.

That's why I think: *Why not take as much joy as possible along the way so when hurt comes, we assimilate it better?*

Every day now I take joy—by refusing to accept the lie that I have to feel miserable about the baggage, the stuff, and the sickness that trails me no matter how I try to hide or outwit it. I choose to do zany, kooky, and funny things to make myself and others laugh.

And I fling joy—beyond my next-door neighbor's fence, clear across town, and into the universe. Then it curves right back to me. Sometimes with a whack on the head when I need it. Sometimes with a thwack into my heart. Sometimes landing with a crack at my feet. But it always comes back. No doubt about it.

Barbara Johnson

Who am I? Me. I'm myself. No other. No duplicate. No clone. God created me, and I'm who He wants me to be. Nothing more. Nothing less. Nothing else. That's true for you, as well.

The writer of Job says each of us has been uniquely shaped by God's hand. He has formed us exactly. The great I Am made us and shaped us. A blessed thought! I don't have to be anybody but me. And as I walk with Christ, he's in the process of making me more like himself. God created us to be who we are and "nothing is to be rejected" (1 Timothy 4:4).

Being who you are is sometimes difficult when you don't like who you are. Accept yourself as God's wonderful creation. Then you are free to be you without fear.

Who are you? God's unique creation. There's nobody just like you. Never has been, never will be. Only you can be you. Be who God made you to be.

Luci Swindoll

Promises About Me

God saw all that he had made, and it was very good.
Genesis 1:31

You created my inmost being;
  you knit me together in my mother's womb.
I praise you because I am fearfully and
     wonderfully made;
  your works are wonderful,
  I know that full well.
My frame was not hidden from you
  when I was made in the secret place.
When I was woven together in the depths of
     the earth,
  your eyes saw my unformed body.
All the days ordained for me
  were written in your book
  before one of them came to be.
     Psalm 139:13–16

Your hands made me and formed me;
  give me understanding.
     Psalm 119:73

Make a Joyful Pit Stop

If you're speeding down the freeway, the police might pull you over. But no one ever makes you take pit stops. You have to choose them. It's the same with life. Emergencies force us to stop, but pit stops of joy are events we plan for and savor.

It's good to let go and bring a little relief into the noise when life is clamoring at you. It won't change any of the circumstances you find yourself in, but when you can laugh at the antics of others, perhaps because you can see yourself in them, that helps to lighten the load.

Does something come to mind for you? It might be a video of family and friends that makes you laugh when watching it. Or maybe it's an old tear-jerker movie with a happy ending.

Whatever makes you feel warm and cozy and helps you celebrate the moment, keep an episode or two at hand and stock up on snacks. There's nothing like a bowl of praline pecan ice cream when the bills are due, the laundry is piled to the ceiling, and the cat just coughed up a fur ball on the dog!

Sheila Walsh

Human beings thrive on laughter. Since most of us can't afford vacations in Hawaii, we have to learn to make our own fun! The best way to do that is to keep your state of mind green and golden: Find, recycle, or produce joy wherever and however you can. A good humorist is a work of heart! The Hasidic Jews believe that the best way to worship God is by being happy. They even incorporate dance and celebration into their spiritual walk.

Humor and laughter are the chocolate chips in the ice cream of life. Remember the old-time "Good Humor man" who drove his ice-cream truck down every street in the neighborhood, chiming a jingle on those hot summer days? All the kids came running as soon as they heard the sound. But good humor doesn't drive down many streets anymore. You have to go out and get it yourself.

Fortunately, it's not that hard to find.

Barbara Johnson

Promises About Joy

He will yet fill your mouth with
laughter
and your lips with shouts
of joy.
                    Job 8:21

Weeping may remain for a night,
but rejoicing comes in the
morning.
              Psalm 30:5

God has brought me laughter, and
everyone who hears about this will
laugh with me.
            Genesis 21:6

Our mouths were filled with
laughter,
our tongues with songs of joy.
Then it was said among the nations,
"The LORD has done great things
for them."
              Psalm 126:2

The Joy All Around Us

Luci, two other dear friends, and I flew to Chile and headed off for what proved to be an off-the-charts, fantastic trip to the Magallenic Penguin Rookery. I wasn't prepared for the utter delight I felt as our bus made its way down to the coastal rookery, carefully threading through hundreds of little penguins who didn't care whose parking lot they were on or how big our bus was.

As we exited the bus, one particularly friendly penguin turned to a woman and began an energetic effort to loosen her shoelaces. When the shoelaces would not yield, the penguin pummeled the woman's leg with a succession of flipper slaps that sent us all into hysterics. The woman was not hurt, but she was sporting some memorable bruises the next day.

To my knowledge, penguins don't serve any useful purpose in life other than to give people like me immense pleasure. From the grandeur of the snow-capped glacier peaks to the awkward land inefficiency of penguins, what fun it is simply to "sing for joy" about God's creation.

Marilyn Meberg

Recently I stopped for breakfast at the local pancake house. I intended to steal a moment to be alone before the day began and its many demands crowded my time.

"Just an egg and a homemade biscuit," I told the waitress. "And a coffee, please." I handed back the menu and turned to the book I'd brought to jump-start my mind.

I had barely finished the second page before she returned with my breakfast. She poured the coffee and asked if there'd be anything else. "No, I'm fine, thank you," I answered.

She smiled. "Enjoy!" she said, then hurried back to deliver someone else's order.

Her final word hung in the air above my corner booth like a blessing. It was a choice she had offered me. I could go through this day oblivious to the miracles all around me, or I could tune in and "enjoy!"

I've heard a lot of sermons in my day, but the best sermon I'd heard in a long time was preached in one word by a busy waitress as she poured a cup of coffee. God has given us this day. I don't want to miss it.

Enjoy!

Gloria Gaither

Promises About the Joy Around Us

*He performs wonders that cannot be
fathomed,
    miracles that cannot be counted.
He bestows rain on the earth;
    he sends water upon the
        countryside.
The lowly he sets on high,
    and those who mourn are lifted to
        safety.*

Job 5:9–11

*Great are the works of the LORD;
    they are pondered by all who
    delight in them.*

Psalm 111:2

*Tell the righteous it will be well with
        them,
    for they will enjoy the fruit of
        their deeds.*

Isaiah 3:10

*My chosen ones will long
        enjoy
    the works of their hands.*

Isaiah 65:22

The Joy of God's Everlasting Love

God's love is a gift that can make you forget yourself at times. The Scottish writer George MacDonald said, "It is the heart that is not yet sure of its God that is afraid to laugh in his presence."

So often with old people and children, all sense of what would be appropriate is swallowed up in what feels right. That's refreshing. We waste too many years between childhood and our older years measuring our behavior on a scale we think we see in someone else's eyes.

God loves us as we are right now! That's one of the things I'm most grateful for. I love the freedom to be myself in God. I pray that a year from now, five years from now, I will be a godlier woman, but I know God won't love me any more than he does right this minute.

Let me tell you, you can run in out of the cold, sit by the fire, put up your feet, and just be yourself. You are loved, you are loved, you are loved!

Sheila Walsh

Do you enjoy hearing tender words from your spouse, children, family, and friends? Of course you do. However, to know that we are loved by an omnipotent, omnipresent, omniscient Lord is the grandest feeling of acceptance anyone can have. When other people fail to express their love to us, we can always depend on Jesus.

Imagine Jesus himself saying to you:

"Child of mine, I love you with an everlasting love. I love you with an unconditional love. I love you because I want to! I love you when others think you are unlovable. I love you when you have sinned and come short of my glory. I love you in the good times and in the bad."

Thelma Wells

Promises About God's Everlasting Love

The LORD appeared to us in the past, saying:
"I have loved you with an everlasting love;
I have drawn you with loving-
kindness."
Jeremiah 31:3

We love because he first loved us.
1 John 4:19

From everlasting to everlasting
the LORD's love is with those who
fear him,
and his righteousness with their
children's children.
Psalm 103:17

Give thanks to the LORD, for he is good;
his love endures forever.
Psalm 118:1

The Joy of God's Creation

One of the things I find fascinating about God's creation is the way he seems to temper the negative environmental elements with corresponding positive ones. For instance, without the nearly ceaseless rains of the Northwest, no incomparable green scenery would greet the eye from all directions. And the snow that snuggles atop Mount Hood, Mount Rainier, and Mount Saint Helens would not exist if, at lower elevations, there were no rain.

By the same token, if God had not created water for the desert environment, it would indeed be an ashtray. But because of water, we have luxuriously green golf courses, languidly swaying palm trees, and even streams in the desert.

God's creative style ensures that something wonderful will offset something less than wonderful. In everything, God seems so balanced.

Marilyn Meberg

Why the gardening mania? Why the books, calendars, accessories, decorations, tools, music, picture frames, furniture, clothes? Why are we so enchanted with white picket fences made into tables and chairs and headboards for the bed? Why the silk grapevines, sweet peas, and ficus trees for the bathroom, kitchen, and hall? Because we crave the sweet serenity of greens and golds and deep brown earth. Because fellowship with God began in a garden, and we long for that time and place. Because leaves quivering in the wind, blossoms nodding, grass ruffled by a breeze, remind us of our real home and the peaceful destiny awaiting us. Because when I cheer up with my geraniums, smile at my pansies, laugh with my petunias, they teach me about God's big greenhouse bursting with joy.

Take the seedlings on loan from heaven and share the growth. Get your gloves muddy, your face tanned, and your knees crinkled here on earth. Nurture faith and love. Keep believing in the harvest. God will make something beautiful out of your effort and energy.

Barbara Johnson

Promises About God's Creation

How many are your works, O LORD!
In wisdom you made them all;
the earth is full of your creatures.

Psalm 104:24

These are but the outer fringe of his works;
how faint the whisper we hear of him!
Who then can understand the thunder
of his power?

Job 26:14

You alone are the LORD. You made
the heavens, even the highest
heavens, and all their starry host,
the earth and all that is on it, the
seas and all that is in them. You
give life to everything, and the
multitudes of heaven worship you.

Nehemiah 9:6

Our Unique Treasures

Men have such a different angle of viewing things than women. We girls call others to come see a playful puppy, a snuggly kitten, or a cooing baby. Meanwhile the guys dangle a grass snake like a charm bracelet, point out the newest road kill, and belch loud enough to register 6.3 on the Richter scale.

That's not to say all guys—just a fair portion—go for the yucky stuff of life. But I find that the he-men in my vicinity would rather investigate a spider's nest than check out the new lace curtains. Even though we did start out in the same garden, we don't seem to be smelling the same rosebush.

We need to respect our differences and value another's contribution. Our differences enable us to enlarge each other's angle of viewing life. Treasure each other's uniqueness and remember to see things from another angle.

Patsy Clairmont

Mother loves to philosophize. "We humans are real pack rats," she once said. "We hold on to the past for dear life." She leaned forward in her chair: "We're not limited just to fine china and snapshots or old leather-bound books. All our lives, we are making collections that are far more significant ... fears, phobias, and suspicions ... hopes, dreams, and illusions ... attributes, persuasions, and prejudices."

As a result of our conversation, I am learning to discard the redundancies of my life. I would be willing to give up nearly every collection I have, except one—my family and friends. They are truly a part of my life that gives me warmth, color, and texture... courage, comfort, and strength... joy, tears, and very often, laughter in large doses!

If I were asked what I cherish most, my answer would surely be my faith in God, but without so much as a comma between, I would have to add my exquisite treasure of friends and family. The simple, basic pleasures of our daily lives are the significant, valuable treasures.

Peggy Benson

Promises About Our Unique Treasures

The body is a unit, though it is made up of many parts; and though all its parts are many, they form one body. So it is with Christ.
1 Corinthians 12:12

There is one body and one Spirit—just as you were called to one hope when you were called—one Lord, one faith, one baptism; one God and Father of all, who is over all and through all and in all. But to each one of us grace has been given as Christ apportioned it.
Ephesians 4:4–7

Just as each of us has one body with many members, and these members do not all have the same function, so in Christ we who are many form one body, and each member belongs to all the others. We have different gifts, according to the grace given us.
Romans 12:4–6

God Is in Control

I see God's fingerprints in his handiwork: a sunrise, a shooting star, a lilac bush, and a newborn's smile. I observe a measure of his strength in a hurricane, an earthquake, a thunderbolt. I see his creativity in a kangaroo, the Grand Canyon, and a blue-eyed, red-headed baby. I detect his humor in a porpoise, a cactus, and a two-year-old's twinkling eyes. I am aware of his mysteriousness when I consider the Trinity, the solar system, and his desire to be in communion with us. "What is man that you are mindful of him?" (Psalm 8:4).

But how do we find God? Sometimes we search him out, and sometimes he "finds" us. Every time we think of God it is because he first had us on his mind. The Lord is always the initiator. He has been from the beginning (Genesis 1:1), and he will be to the end (Revelation 1:7). So know that once you have invited him to enter your life, you are on his mind and he is in your heart.

Patsy Clairmont

When I say "The Lord is my shepherd,"
I remember that he has charge over my
life. As my shepherd, he watches over me
to see that I stay in the fold. He loves me
unconditionally in spite of my going my own
willful way sometimes. He protects me from
danger. He provides everything for me. He
chastises me when I do wrong. He comforts
me when I am distressed. He bandages
my wounds when I get hurt. He calms my
fears when I am afraid. He takes care of my
relationships when they become shaky. He
bathes me in his Spirit when I seek his face.
He communicates with me in ways I can
understand.

God promises to provide all our needs
according to his riches in glory in Christ
Jesus. I know he will do that. And he
delights in often giving us what we want,
too.

You can depend on him to watch over
you, to protect you, to provide for you,
to comfort you, to chastise you when you
need it, to bandage your wounds, to calm
your fears, to care for your relationships,
to communicate with you, and to love you
unconditionally.

Thelma Wells

He who did not spare his own Son, but gave him up for us all—how will he not also, along with him, graciously give us all things?
Romans 8:32

My God will meet all your needs according to his glorious riches in Christ Jesus.
Philippians 4:19

Keep your lives free from the love of money and be content with what you have, because God has said,
"Never will I leave you;
never will I forsake you."
So we say with confidence,
"The Lord is my helper; I will not
be afraid."
Hebrews 13:5–6

The Lord is my light and my salvation—
whom shall I fear?
The Lord is the stronghold of my life—
of whom shall I be afraid?
Psalm 27:1

The Joy of God's Gifts

Our God is a gift giver. His generosity is obvious in how lavishly he bestows on us rainbows, waterfalls, canyons, and white caps.

One day when I was visiting the desert, a marshmallow cloud formation drizzled over the mountaintop like so much whipped cream. I brought my bike to a standstill and just beheld this delicious scene for thirty-five minutes. Another evening, the sunset turned the skyline into a saucer of peaches and cream—absolutely dreamy. The Lord serves up his scrumptious beauty in liberal portions and then invites us to partake.

I have often joined Marilyn Meberg at nightfall for the spectacular performance as the sun sets. The mountains go through a series of thrilling changes. From pinks to lavenders to deep purples, the setting sun and emerging evening appear to cover the hillside for sleep. Marilyn and I never tire of the Lord's thrilling displays. We "ooh!" and "aah!" in all the right places, and we can feel our blood pressure balancing out as smiles and giggles of pleasure help us to express our gratitude.

Patsy Clairmont

Our support group has met monthly in a church across from Disneyland. During the summer months, the 9:30 P.M. fireworks over Disneyland always interrupt our meetings. I'd usually get irritated and annoyed until one evening a couple from Iowa joined us. As soon as the fireworks started, they sat up, eyes twinkling. "Oh, the fireworks!" they exclaimed. There was wonder in their faces. They were excited and suddenly animated. "Can we stop for a few minutes to watch them?" they asked.

Think of everything you normally take for granted. Make a list of the most ordinary, tedious things that happen every day over and over in your life. Now imagine a homeless man or woman coming to live with you for a day. What do you think they would say about the linens and soft blankets? The furnace that blows heat through the floor?

"Oh, the fireworks!" The marvelous kingdom of our God is right across the street regardless of where we live. We may as well get enthused and infect everyone we meet with his amazing love and power. Let the fireworks begin!

Barbara Johnson

Promises About God's Gifts

Every good and perfect gift is from above, coming down from the Father of the heavenly lights, who does not change like shifting shadows.

James 1:17

Who gave man his mouth? Who makes him deaf or mute? Who gives him sight or makes him blind? Is it not I, the LORD? Now go; I will help you speak and will teach you what to say.

Exodus 4:11–12

If you, then, though you are evil, know how to give good gifts to your children, how much more will your Father in heaven give good gifts to those who ask him!

Matthew 7:11

The Joy of Good Friends

Sometimes, when I can't sleep, I lie in bed, and instead of counting sheep, I count all the fun people God has put in my life.

On one such occasion, I'd gone to bed at 10:30 P.M. When I woke up, I was sure it must be morning and was shocked to see that the clock on my bedside table said it was only 12:30 A.M. I slipped out of bed, went downstairs, made some hot tea, and switched on the TV. But when the clock said it was 3:30 A.M., I went back upstairs, determined to fall asleep.

That's when I remembered some of the stories Luci, Patsy, and Marilyn tell when they speak at the conferences, and I started to laugh. I don't know if you've ever felt like laughing while the person next to you is fast asleep, but it makes you laugh even more. I stuck my head under the covers to try to muffle my snorts.

Who can make you giggle and snort under the covers just by thinking about them and their antics? The next time you can't sleep, thank God for all those who make your life richer!

Sheila Walsh

Like people, plants are born with personality. The difference, I think, is that in his plan for people, God added humor!

Some plants feed upon a seed beneath the earth. Others push the seed case forth—some with methodical care, others with reckless abandonment.

I am often gently nourished by a friend whose quiet company provides wisdom and comfort for my spirit.

I am sometimes coquettishly coaxed from my comfortable environment and persistently urged through the crusty surface soil by friends.

But, on occasion, I have been catapulted from my warm bed to worlds beyond my experience by the likes of my professional colleagues or family members.

We nurture and are nourished by our friends in different ways. In his plan for friends, I think God often paints way outside the lines. The color may not rival that of the flower garden, but the comedy is superb!

Joy MacKenzie

*A friend loves at all times,
    and a brother is born for
        adversity.*
            Proverbs 17:17

Jesus said, "I no longer call you servants,
because a servant does not know his
master's business. Instead, I have called you
friends, for everything that I learned from my
Father I have made known to you."
            John 15:15

*Perfume and incense bring joy to the heart,
    and the pleasantness of one's friend
        springs from his earnest counsel.*
            Proverbs 27:9

*Two are better than one,
    because they have a good
        return for their work:
If one falls down,
    his friend can help him up.*
            Ecclesiastes 4:9–10

Secure in God's Love

How does one find God? He is in our prayers guiding our words, he is in our songs as we worship him, and he is filling our mouths when we comfort a friend or speak wisdom to someone who needs hope. Sometimes we can search so hard for the miraculous we miss the obvious reality of his ever-present nearness. Count your blessings. He is in them, too.

We can't command the Lord into our awareness. He is King; we are his beloved subjects. When our hearts are tenderly responsive ("Whatever, Lord") and it suits his greater plan, then the Lord will lift the thin veil that separates us. And we will be stunned to realize that he has been closer than our own breath all along.

By the way, it has been my experience that I keep refinding him, which has helped to define me. You, too, may lose track of your faith. Remember, it is never too late to step back on the path.

Patsy Clairmont

My baby boy has no sense of what's appropriate on the noise-making front. On the first Sunday we took him to church, we opted to sit in the back row, knowing that at the first squawk we could be up and out fast. As the sermon started, everything seemed fine. Christian was cuddled up in my arms, deep in sleep, or so I thought. Suddenly, Christian burst into a baby version of "Moon River" at a decibel level that could have burst a dog's eardrums. I jumped up so quickly I nearly dropped him. I hurried out, whispering "Shh!" vainly in his ear. That only seemed to encourage him, and he moved into verse two, grinning from ear to ear.

By the time we were outside, I was laughing so hard I could barely walk or breathe. There is something so charming about that kind of innocence. When children are secure, they feel free to be who they really are. That's how you and I can live, too. God is the only one who knows everything about us. He knows it all, and he loves you. What a gift in a world where there is so much uncertainty!

Sheila Walsh

Promises About God's Love

God so loved the world that he gave his one and only Son, that whoever believes in him shall not perish but have eternal life.
John 3:16

God demonstrates his own love for us in this: While we were still sinners, Christ died for us.
Romans 5:8

*I love those who love me,
    and those who seek me find me.*
Proverbs 8:17

We know and rely on the love God has for us. God is love. Whoever lives in love lives in God, and God in him.
1 John 4:16

A Joyful Child of God

Early Christmas morning! Waking up in a cold bedroom, frost on the windowpanes, snow draping the trees outside my window. Wrapping up in warm dressing gowns and slippers. Creeping down the stairs barely able to contain the excitement. Opening the living-room door ... a wonderland, a transformation overnight from the ordinary to every unspoken wish laid out in gold and red and green packages. Tangerines wrapped in silver paper. The aroma of turkey filling every room.

I wonder why our vision becomes impaired with the turning of calendar pages. We have forgotten what joy looks like. We were made for joy, but we have forgotten what it smells like. We've forgotten how it sounds.

Before you go to bed tonight, do one thing that will bring back a little joy from childhood. Have some cookies and milk or throw a duckie in your bath. Buy a children's book and curl up by the fire and read. Welcome to ... joy!

Sheila Walsh

I love playful people! People who aren't too sophisticated or too proper to engage in zany antics draw me like a two-year-old to mud.

Sometimes I think we responsible adults assume that being playful might be interpreted as being childish, maybe even silly. Admittedly, nothing is more tragic than an adult who fails to gain the maturity and wisdom necessary to live a productive life. But equally tragic are adults who forget how to vent their play instincts.

The mature person is able to recognize the distinction between the two worlds and choose which world is appropriate for the moment.

Jesus said it's impossible to enter the kingdom unless we become as little children (Mark 10:15). He seemed to place a high premium on that childlike quality. He reminds us of how preferable it is at times to be childlike.

Marilyn Meberg

To all who received him, to those who believed in his name, he gave the right to become children of God—children born not of natural descent, nor of human decision or a husband's will, but born of God.

John 1:12–13

Do everything without complaining or arguing, so that you may become blameless and pure, children of God without fault in a crooked and depraved generation, in which you shine like stars in the universe.

Philippians 2:14–15

How great is the love the Father has lavished on us, that we should be called children of God! And that is what we are!

1 John 3:1

Joyful Companions

Given first dibs on travel companions, I would pick Thelma, Luci, Marilyn, Sheila, and Barbara right off the bat.

Thelma often is tucked in a corner behind the scenes, Bible spread open, preparing herself for ministry.

Luci can guide us into stimulating conversations as well with her witty, thought-provoking questions.

Marilyn keeps us all chortling and challenged with her comedic sense and her insightful offerings.

Sheila's brilliant mind, lightning-quick humor, and sterling devotion brighten my path.

Barbara's a seasoned journeyer who has taught me how to travel on with smiles in my miles.

Who are your traveling chums? Do they promote smiles in your miles? Do they add joy to your journey? When we choose companions may we be wise and select those who are wholesome, humorous, helpful, and honorable.

Patsy Clairmont

One of my favorite early spring flowers is the Johnny-jump-up. It is a first cousin to the pansy. They have sweet smiling faces, each with its own personality. Each morning, the sweet smiling faces of these small flowers look up at me as they settle their roots into the earth.

I smile back as I see in them the faces of my "jump-up" friends—people who have come into my life over the years at just the exact time I needed to see a friendly, smiling face. They are people who believe in me and let me know it in many ways. They are quick to send a note of encouragement, make a phone call, or surprise me with a birthday gift. What a tremendous rescue team!

During the days of spring, as I walk into my garden and think and pray about my life—where I've been and where I might be next—I smile to myself and remember, and I thank God for all of my Johnny-jump-ups!

Peggy Benson

Promises About Joyful Companions

Shout for joy to the LORD, all the earth.
Worship the LORD with gladness;
  come before him with joyful songs.
Know that the LORD is God.
  It is he who made us, and we are his;
  we are his people, the sheep of his
    pasture.

Psalm 100:1–3

If two lie down together, they will
  keep warm.
  But how can one keep warm
    alone?
Though one may be overpowered,
  two can defend themselves.
A cord of three strands is not quickly
  broken.

Ecclesiastes 4:11–12

Ruth replied, "Don't urge me to leave you
or to turn back from you. Where you go I
will go, and where you stay I will stay. Your
people will be my people and your God my
God. Where you die I will die, and there I will
be buried."

Ruth 1:16–17

God Always Remembers

Christi at New Life Clinics asked me to be the surprise guest for the employees at their annual Christmas dinner. I agreed. But I didn't write it down.

The day of the event, I kept feeling this annoying tug that said, *You're supposed to do something today.* But I couldn't think of what it was.

On Christmas Day someone asked me how the surprise appearance at New Life had worked out. Oh, no! My heart was sick. I forced myself to face up to what I had done.

Wouldn't it be horrible if Jesus were so busy he couldn't remember what we talked to him about?

Thank God we don't have to endure that kind of treatment from our Lord! Hallelujah, we are never forgotten! God can be depended on. We disappoint loved ones. We inconvenience people we care about. But how wonderful, how beautiful, how comforting to know we have a God who is always near to console and cheer, just when we need him most.

Thelma Wells

Les and I were in an antique shop the other day when we spotted a photo album on a table. Interested, we peeked inside only to find a family peering back at us.

We both felt sad seeing someone's snapshots cast aside for strangers to peruse. We wondered who would throw away his or her history (a few family members maybe, but the whole clan)? How does one toss out a picture without guilt? A person's likeness is so personal it seems like a violation to discard them. After all, what if these individuals have rejection issues? And who would purpose to buy more relatives?

Ever feel like your identity is lost in a world full of people? We have a God whose heart is expansive enough to hold us all and yet who's so intently focused on each of us that he knows our rising up and our sitting down. Our faces are no surprise to the Lord, and our identities are engraved in the palms of his hands.

Patsy Clairmont

Can a mother forget the baby at her
    breast
  and have no compassion on the
    child she has borne?
Though she may forget,
  I will not forget you!
    Isaiah 49:15

God is not unjust; he will not forget
your work and the love you have
shown him as you have helped his
people and continue to help them.
    Hebrews 6:10

Only be careful, and watch yourselves closely
so that you do not forget the things your
eyes have seen or let them slip from your
heart as long as you live. Teach them to your
children and to their children after them.
    Deuteronomy 4:9

Get wisdom, get understanding;
    do not forget my words or swerve
      from them.
        Proverbs 4:5

The Joy of God's Touch

I was a guest singer at a Billy Graham crusade. Billy's message was simple and uncompromising. No bells or whistles "wowed" the crowd, just a simple call was made to "come home." I wondered what the response would be. I wondered if the message sounded too good to be true. I wondered if it sounded too simple.

But then it began. People began to stream to the front to receive Christ. I had to bury my face in my hands, overwhelmed with pure joy at being a spectator to such a homecoming.

It would be such a shame to sit in church every Sunday and listen to what's being said about God but never grasp that this is a personal invitation—a welcome mat just for you.

"If we confess our sins, he is faithful and just and will forgive us our sins and purify us from all unrighteousness" (1 John 1:9). Isn't that great? Isn't that simple? All you have to do is pray:

"Father, thank you that you love me. Thank you that Jesus died for me. I want to come home. Thank you for waiting for me. Amen."

Sheila Walsh

We want and need to know who we are. Of course, for the believer, there need not be a puzzle. Specific attention, thought, and planning about me took place before God actually formed me in the womb. That implies I am much more than a cozy encounter between my parents nine months before I was born. No matter the circumstances surrounding my conception, I am a planned event.

Not only am I a planned event, I was "set apart." I have a specific task to do for God. We all have a specific task to do for God, and it was planned in his head before we were ever formed in the womb. That is an incredible truth!

Not only is my identity and calling known, but as Isaiah 43:1 says, "I have called you by name; you are Mine!" (NASB). He considers me unique and set apart, and he calls me his own.

May we sink into that cushion of joyful peace and never forget "whose we be."

Marilyn Meberg

Promises About God's Touch

This is what the LORD says:
"Fear not, for I have redeemed you;
    I have summoned you by name; you
        are mine."
            Isaiah 43:1

I will do the very thing you have
asked, because I am pleased with
you and I know you by name.
    Exodus 33:17

I, the LORD, have called you in righteousness;
    I will take hold of your hand.
        Isaiah 42:6

I will refine them like silver
    and test them like gold.
They will call on my name
    and I will answer them;
I will say, "They are my people,"
    and they will say, "The LORD is our
God."
        Zechariah 13:9

A Joyful Up-Look

The Joy of Change

Like it or not, constant change is part of modern life. What in the world doesn't change?

1. God's love.

2. Friendship with his Son.

3. The power of the Holy Spirit.

When you think you've had just about all the change you can stand, reach out and take one step further into God's wide arms. Though his love, friendship, and power never change, he made you with a big, elastic spiritual cord that stretches with every tug and pull. He knows exactly how much give it's got. If he's calling you to stretch, he knows you've got what it takes. Reach! You'll become more confident and enthusiastic about life if you do.

God knows change can make your life richer. Live for today, but hold your hands open to tomorrow. Anticipate the future and its changes with joy. There is a seed of God's love in every event, every circumstance, every unpleasant situation in which you may find yourself. Don't get stuck in a rut or hung up on an outdated blessing. You serve a God of change!

Barbara Johnson

Change! You can count on it! Life boasts very few things that are absolutely dependable, but change is one of them, and it is the one we seem to fear most.

The moon and the ocean both provide exquisite models of the rhythm of life: consistent in their waxing and waning, advance and retreat, ebb and flow. But in our brief earthly journey, most of us just haven't quite been able to get the hang of it. We dread the ebbing, fearing the flow will never return. We demand a constancy that is impossible.

If the joy is in the flow—the moments of great advance, the rush—then the maturing and growing is in the retreat—the pulling back, the ebb—during which there is a grand preparation and anticipation of the next exciting surge forward. The mighty ocean wave retreats to empower its next forward motion.

In God's infinite understanding of the human condition, he reaches out to assuage the dread and fear of change: Trust me, he says. I will never leave you. Come to me ... and I will give you rest. In my presence is fullness of joy.

Joy MacKenzie

Promises About Change

You have made known to me
the path of life;
you will fill me with joy in
your presence,
with eternal pleasures at
your right hand.
Psalm 16:11

There is a time for everything,
and a season for every activity
under heaven:
a time to be born and a time to die,
a time to plant and a time to uproot,
a time to kill and a time to heal,
a time to tear down and a time to build,
a time to weep and a time to laugh,
a time to mourn and a time to dance,
a time to scatter stones and a time to
gather them,
a time to embrace and a time to refrain,
a time to search and a time to give up,
a time to keep and a time to throw
away,
a time to tear and a time to mend,
a time to be silent and a time to speak,
a time to love and a time to hate,
a time for war and a time for peace.
Ecclesiastes 3:1–8

Finding Hope in Jesus

I attended a gala occasion recently to which I wore a dressy pants outfit with stylish heels. My hair was fluffed, and my ears were adorned with a new pair of dazzling earrings. I felt spiffy ... until I arrived at the event. I was the only woman with slacks on, and I felt awkward. After a considerable time, I spotted another gal in slacks, and I wondered if she would want to sit with me and be best friends. Soon several others arrived in similar attire, and I no longer felt the need to bond.

Aren't we funny? We work hard to be originals and then fear our originality has made us different. I enjoy being center stage unless it's under a critical spotlight. Like the time I spoke only to learn afterward that my slip was hanging in a southerly direction, waving to the onlookers. Following the sessions, several hundred women alerted me so I could hike it up. Believe me, I wanted to take a hike ... an exceedingly long one to another land. Despite today's fads, I prefer to keep my underwear undercover. Know what I mean?

Patsy Clairmont

The ocean is a favorite place of mine. I love to listen to sounds that only the waves can make. I walk miles along the shoreline leaving my footprints in the sand, which are then invaded by an endless ebb and flow of the tide. These moments bring an unspeakable calm. I can see with a clear mind and heart all the ways God has held my life and walked me through the violent storms to bring me to a restful place. Even the bad memories—those painful reminders of hurt and disappointment—somehow get covered with sweet forgiveness and a yearning for all to be right and true under the warm blanket of the LORD's mercy.

It is when my mind is stayed on Jesus, when my eyes look toward eternal things, when my ears listen way beyond the voices of the day, that I hear the ocean sing. The LORD miraculously puts everything into his perspective when my mind and heart are set on all that he is, on all that he's done, on all that he's promised. I become more thankful, I become more hopeful, and most importantly, I am humbled.

Kathy Troccoli

Promises About Hope in Jesus

Surely God is my salvation;
I will trust and not be afraid.
The Lord, the Lord, is my strength and
my song;
he has become my salvation.
Isaiah 12:2

I am not ashamed, because I know whom I have believed, and am convinced that he is able to guard what I have entrusted to him for that day.
2 Timothy 1:12

Jesus said, "Do not let your hearts be troubled. Trust in God; trust also in me."
John 14:1

May the God of hope fill you with all joy and peace as you trust in him, so that you may overflow with hope by the power of the Holy Spirit.
Romans 15:13

No Regrets

Did you know that an opal is a stone with a broken heart? Made of dust, sand, and silica, it is full of minute fissures that allow air to be trapped inside. The trapped air refracts the light, resulting in the lovely hues that inspire the opal's nickname, the Lamp of Fire. When kept in a cold, dark place, the opal loses its luster. But when held in a warm hand or when the light shines on it, the luster is restored. So it is with us. A broken heart becomes a lamp of fire when we allow God to breathe on it and warm us with his life.

If things are tough, remember that every flower that ever bloomed had to go through a whole lot of dirt to get there. The Almighty Father will use life's reverses to move you forward. So do not keep grieving about a bitter experience. The present is slipping by while you are regretting the past and worrying about the future. Regret will not prevent tomorrow's sorrows; it will only rob today of its strength. So keep on believing. with Jesus you do not have a hopeless end but an endless hope!

Barbara Johnson

Ever wish you could start over? Probably all of us have longed for another chance in some area of our lives. We wouldn't necessarily have done things differently, just more or perhaps less.

The truth is, we can't go backward, only forward into uncharted territory. To sit in our sorrow would lead to misery. Although regret that leads to change is a dear friend, regret that leads to shame is a treacherous enemy.

There is, no guarantee that if we had done a part of our lives differently, things would end any differently. We have to trust the God of the universe who directs the outcome of all things that he will do that which ultimately needs to be done.

Many things are now out of our control, but never his. So the next time you and I need something to lean on, let's make it the LORD.

Patsy Clairmont

Promises About Regret

Godly sorrow brings repentance that leads to salvation and leaves no regret, but worldly sorrow brings death.

2 Corinthians 7:10

Repent! Turn away from all your offenses; then sin will not be your downfall. Rid yourselves of all the offenses you have committed, and get a new heart and a new spirit.

Ezekiel 18:30–31

When God saw what they did and how they turned from their evil ways, he had compassion and did not bring upon them the destruction he had threatened.

Jonah 3:10

Repent, then, and turn to God, so that your sins may be wiped out, that times of refreshing may come from the LORD.

Acts 3:19

Joy Sappers

Some say truth is stranger than fiction; others say it isn't stranger, just more rare. (One thing is sure: If you tell the truth, there's less to remember!)

No matter what, don't ever let yesterday use up too much of today. f it sneaks up on you, turn the tables on it. Like interest rates, make trouble work for you, not against you. You don't always need a comedian to make you laugh. Once you get started, you can pull a few one-liners out of the bag yourself. When someone says, "Life is hard," say, "I prefer it to the alternative, don't you?" When somebody else complains about getting old, answer, "Right now, I'm just sitting here being thankful that wrinkles don't hurt!"

Life is too short to spend it being angry, bored, or dull. That was never God's intention. Maybe boredom and dullness aren't on any list of sins in the Bible, but they will sap your joy if you tolerate them.

Barbara Johnson

Did you mail that insurance form, sweetie?" I asked Barry one afternoon.

He seemed to lose a little color. "I forgot," he said.

"Why would you forget something as important as that?" I snapped.

"I'm sorry, honey. I just forgot," he said.

I found myself standing on the edge of a cliff and knew I had to choose whether I would dive off or back off. I asked Barry to excuse me for a moment, and I made a conscious, determined choice to get on my knees and to let my anger go. As I released my fury, I was filled with joy.

Choosing to let go of my tempestuous responses may not seem big to you, but it's making a huge difference in our lives. I want to be the fragrance of Christ in the midst of the storms of life, not part of the storm front.

If you struggle with old behaviors that are as familiar to you as the spider veins on your legs, I encourage you to invite Christ into the moment and to let those old patterns go. You can choose. You can be a drip of rain or a ray of sunshine.

Sheila Walsh

Promises About Joy
Sappers

Take note of this: Everyone should be quick to listen, slow to speak and slow to become angry.

James 1:19

Your attitude should be the same as that of Christ Jesus:
*Who, being in very nature God,
did not consider equality with
God something to be grasped,
but made himself nothing,
taking the very nature of a
servant.*
Philippians 2:5–7

Jesus said, "Take my yoke upon you and learn from me, for I am gentle and humble in heart, and you will find rest for your souls."

Matthew 11:29

Whoever claims to live in him must walk as Jesus did.

1 John 2:6

Soaring Through Struggles

I was flying from Minneapolis to California, or so I thought, when the pilot announced we were returning to our port of departure. *Whatever for?* we all wondered, groaning and complaining. The pilot explained that the aircraft couldn't get enough altitude to clear the Rocky Mountains near Denver. Despite our mutterings, we turned around and headed back.

Once on the ground, it wasn't long before the airplane mechanics found the problem. One of them had left a vacuum hose in the door, preventing the seal from being tight enough to allow the cabin to be pressurized and thus enable the plane to clear the Rockies. A simple error by a careless mechanic drained the airplane's power to soar.

What's your personal vacuum hose that keeps you from soaring? Pray for illumination. Let go of worry. Follow the disciplines outlined in the Bible. Communicate with the Pilot as well as the ground crew. Do whatever is necessary to remove the hoses that drain your energy or force you backward. Don't give up and take the bus. It's better to fly. Remember that underneath are the "everlasting arms."

Barbara Johnson

Defying odds, breaking barriers, not being held back. I know people like that. They're a source of encouragement to me. They hang tough when others give up, forge ahead when others lag behind, choose to be cheerful when others sink in defeat.

Yet even more powerful are the words of Jesus, who challenged his followers to move mountains, walk on water, and prepare a picnic for five thousand. He assured us we would do no less than the impossible.

I don't know the circumstances of your life. Maybe you're experiencing a financial crisis, a relational struggle, or a genuine feeling of inadequacy. Whatever your biggest problems, be sure you aren't surrendering to the odds. You may look at yourself and say, "I can't. I can't rise above this, get beyond it, or overcome," and so you give up. Let me say with all the love in the world, my friend, don't quit. You're just starting this ride. You have the whole sky above your head. God wants to free you from bondage, and he knows just how to do it.

Luci Swindoll

Promises About Soaring Through Struggles

Even to your old age and gray hairs
I am he, I am he who will sustain you.
I have made you and I will carry you;
I will sustain you and I will
rescue you.
Isaiah 46:4

The eternal God is your refuge,
and underneath are the everlasting
arms.
Deuteronomy 33:27

He knows the way that I take;
when he has tested me, I will
come forth as gold.
Job 23:10

For a little while you may have had to suffer grief in all kinds of trials. These have come so that your faith—of greater worth than gold, which perishes even though refined by fire—may be proved genuine and may result in praise, glory and honor when Jesus Christ is revealed.

1 Peter 1:6–7

The Joy of Persevering

A calmer faith. That's the quiet place
within us where we don't get whiplash every
time life tosses us a curve. Where we don't
revolt when his plan and ours conflict. Where
we relax (versus stew, sweat, and swear) in
the midst of an answerless season. Where we
accept (and expect) deserts in our spiritual
journey as surely as we do joy. Where we
are not intimidated or persuaded by other
people's agendas, but moved only by him.
Where we weep in repentance, sleep in
peace, live in fullness, and sing of victory.

Patsy Clairmont

My daughter Vikki, with her free spirit, discovered that once you start to climb a mountain, it's so steep and rough your only option is to keep your sights on finishing and your mind on the rocks and boulders up ahead. You have to keep looking forward and not back, and you have to pray every step of the way that you will make it.

The road to glory is difficult with its rocks and boulders, its strain and struggle. Things aren't always as easy as we would like. Surprises and pitfalls wait for us along the road of life. We're going to sweat and sway, we're going to wonder why things are the way they are.

But every road has an end; every mountain has its peak. If we can just hold on and keep climbing, knowing that God is aware of how we're straining, he will bring us up and over the mountains. It's consoling to know God is in control of every part of our journey to glory, even over the steep mountains.

Thelma Wells

Promises About Persevering

Jesus said, "To him who overcomes, I will give the right to eat from the tree of life, which is in the paradise of God."
Revelation 2:7

Let us not become weary in doing good, for at the proper time we will reap a harvest if we do not give up.
Galatians 6:9

To those who by persistence in doing good seek glory, honor and immortality, God will give eternal life.
Romans 2:7

Stand firm. Let nothing move you. Always give yourselves fully to the work of the LORD, because you know that your labor in the LORD is not in vain.
1 Corinthians 15:58

The Joy of a Godly Perspective

Charles Darrow didn't set out to become a millionaire when he developed "Monopoly," the game that was later marketed around the world by Parker Brothers, but that's what happened. The little gift he developed from scraps of cardboard and tiny pieces of wood was simply a way to keep his wife's spirits up during her Depression-era pregnancy. Darrow created a gift of joy, shared it with the world, and the gift came right back to him a thousandfold.

Are times tough in your little apartment—or lavish mansion? Are you weary from standing in lines that lead to nowhere? If it seems as if your world is collapsing around you or you feel yourself slipping down into the depths of depression, don't despair.

Remember that the right temperature in a home is maintained by warm hearts, not by icy glares, lukewarm enthusiasm—or hotheads! Your attitude can set the tone for your whole family. So use whatever scraps you can find—even if, in the beginning, it's just a scrap of a smile, then watch the gifts come back to you.

Barbara Johnson

Life is a process. To God, process isn't a means to an end; it is the goal. Whatever sends us running to him, makes us embrace him, causes us to depend on him, is the best good in our lives.

We have been at times so full of gratitude and awe that we haven't been able to do anything else but sing, "Let's just praise the LORD." At other times, we haven't been able to see how God could possibly be there in the dark circumstances of life, yet we have learned that he was always—in all things—up to something good in our lives. That "good" is always eternal good.

Some of life's circumstances seem senseless, and others, too painful to bear. But when we base our confidence on a perspective broader than this world's view, we can trust that what our sovereign God is working to accomplish is not the servant of this world's circumstances; rather, this world's circumstances are always being made the servant of his purposes.

Let's just praise the LORD!

Gloria Gaither

"For I know the plans I have for you,"
declares the LORD, "plans to prosper you and
not to harm you, plans to give you hope and
a future."

Jeremiah 29:11

"For my thoughts are not your thoughts,
neither are your ways my ways,"
declares the LORD.
"As the heavens are higher than
the earth,
so are my ways higher than
your ways
and my thoughts than your thoughts."
Isaiah 55:8–9

Oh, the depth of the riches of the
wisdom and knowledge of God!
How unsearchable his judgments,
and his paths beyond tracing out!
"Who has known the mind of the LORD?
Or who has been his counselor?"
"Who has ever given to God,
that God should repay him?"
For from him and through him and to
him are all things.
To him be the glory forever! Amen.
Romans 11:33–36

The Joy of Possibilities

Though the fig tree should not blossom,
And there be no fruit on the vines,
Though the yield of the olive should fail,
And the fields produce no food,
Though the flock should be cut off from the
    fold,
And there be no cattle in the stalls,
Yet I will exult in the LORD,
I will rejoice in the God of my salvation.
The LORD God is my strength,
And He has made my feet like hinds' feet,
And makes me walk on my high places."
                    Habbukuk 3:17–19 NASB

The LORD is my strength and my shield;
    my heart trusts in him, and I am helped.
My heart leaps for joy
    and I will give thanks to him in song.
                    Psalm 28:7

I will sing of your strength,
    in the morning I will sing of your love;
for you are my fortress,
    my refuge in times of trouble.
                    Psalm 59:16

There are moments in the harsh bleakness of winter that would be unbearable if there were not, tucked deep within its bosom, the promise of spring. But spring always comes. Dark moments in the life and heart of a mother or wife are mitigated only in the light of God's sovereignty. We must learn to draw upon the resources of a sovereign God—One who unreservedly offers us not solutions, not answers, not happily-ever-after endings, but his glad welcome—the assurance of his presence with us.

The desert has its edge, and in God's timing the darkness will give way to light. Ephesians 3:12 is our warranty: "We may approach God with freedom and confidence." Assured of his glad welcome, we can take our places in a world full of people like ourselves—people who don't know where to turn, who never in a million years expected to find themselves in their present circumstances—people for whom there are no answers but Jesus Christ. And we can do it joyfully!

Joy MacKenzie

Promises About Possibilities

Everyone born of God overcomes the world. This is the victory that has overcome the world, even our faith.

1 John 5:4

Jesus said, "I have told you these things, so that in me you may have peace. In this world you will have trouble. But take heart! I have overcome the world."

John 16:33

with God all things are possible.

Matthew 19:26

Sovereign LORD, you have made the heavens and the earth by your great power and outstretched arm. Nothing is too hard for you.

Jeremiah 32:17

The Joy of Trusting God's Plan

Look at the life you hold in your own two hands. Is it tattered and shabby? Think about it. Might it bring opportunities for growth and gladness? What is going to be important one hundred years from now that doesn't seem important now? What seems important now that will not be important a century from now?

In moments that appear unredeemable, watch and wait. Recognize the precious things. Refuse to trash anything! Ask God to help you see things from his perspective. Take one step after another. Before long, in spite of yourself, you may notice surprising signs of hope in your own backyard.

Trial and triumph are what God uses to scribble all over the pages of our lives. They are signs that he is using us, loving us, shaping us to his image, enjoying our companionship, delivering us from evil, and writing eternity into our hearts. Be happy through everything because today is the only thing you can be sure of. Right here, right now, cherish the moment you hold in your hands.

Barbara Johnson

In God's infinite plan for my life, he allowed me to be born out of wedlock to a crippled girl whose parents were so embarrassed by the situation they forced her to leave their home and find her own way. My great- grandmother convinced my mother to let me live at Granny's house. Granny and my great-grandfather, Daddy Harrell, became very attached to me. Daddy Harrell and I became best friends. He was blind, but as soon as I was old enough to learn my way around the neighborhood, I became his eyes. I held his hand and led him down the street to the doctor's office, to visit his friends, or to church.

Just as Daddy Harrell trusted me to lead him from place to place without fear of falling or being run over by a car, he taught me to trust God by turning over to him my fears and anxieties. God knew my great-grandparents' nurturing would be the catalyst that would propel me to learn the truths about who God is and how he works in our everyday lives. I know my heavenly Father because I have seen him in the people I love.

Thelma Wells

Promises About Trusting God's Plan

It is not for you to know the times or dates the Father has set by his own authority.
Acts 1:7

Those who know your name will trust in you,
for you, LORD, have never forsaken
those who seek you.
Psalm 9:10

Blessed is the man who trusts in the LORD,
whose confidence is in him.
He will be like a tree planted by the water
that sends out its roots by the stream.
It does not fear when heat comes;
its leaves are always green.
It has no worries in a year of drought
and never fails to bear fruit.
Jeremiah 17:7–8

Fear the LORD, you his saints,
for those who fear him lack
nothing.
Psalm 34:9

Standing with Others in Prayer

Anytime we stop to be present with others in their trouble, we carry the opportunity to bring boomerang joy. You don't have to be famous or important. You don't have to be acclaimed or much sought after. Just be you. Stay true to yourself and those values that keep you grounded in kindness.

Keep looking for the boomerang surprise in your life. Listen for the whirring sound that means it may be getting close. Always stay connected to people and seek out things that bring you joy. Dream with abandon. Pray confidently. But be careful what you pray for—because everything and anything is possible through the power of prayer!

Barbara Johnson

As a mother, I find solace in praying for my children during the good times and the bad. To help my children and myself to get focused on how to deal with problems, I ask my children if they have listened to praise music before they called to tell me about their woes. If they haven't, I ask them to call back after they have—unless, of course, it's an emergency.

I believe one of the best ways to get in a praying mood is to listen to music that ushers you into a spirit of adoration. That, in turn, takes your mind off the problem and helps you to focus on the Problem-Solver.

While I wait for them to call back, I follow my own instructions. I sing, listen to gospel music, and pray. Usually, when they phone me again, both of us are in harmony with each other and the LORD.

We are admonished to pray without ceasing because prayers assert God's power in our lives. Even our unuttered thoughts can be prayers, which enables us to pray without ceasing. When we fail to pray, we aren't cheating God; we're cheating ourselves.

Thelma Wells

Promises About Standing with Others in Prayer

The LORD says, "Call to me and I will answer you and tell you great and unsearchable things you do not know."
Jeremiah 33:3

The LORD is near to all who call on him,
to all who call on him in truth.
Psalm 145:18

Jesus said, "And I will do whatever you ask in my name, so that the Son may bring glory to the Father. You may ask me for anything in my name, and I will do it."
John 14:13–14

Carry each other's burdens, and in this way you will fulfill the law of Christ.
Galatians 6:2

The Joy of God's Great Faithfulness

Christians sometimes have more trouble handling trouble than the world does, because we think we should be perfect. As things veer out of control, you may find yourself asking, "Who stopped payment on my reality check?"

Too often our faith is shallow. We cling to the padded cross instead of the "old rugged cross" of the hymn. What should set us apart is our trust, our ability to let God loose in our circumstances rather than forever trying to control them ourselves.

Admit it and save yourself years of worry. There are no superfamilies. There are no perfect people. You are right where "X marks the spot" on the map of life. Whatever dilemma you're facing, ask yourself what difference it will make one hundred years from today. The difference is in letting go and letting God. He'll never let you down. He'll help you face tomorrow with open hands, open heart, open mind, and tons of confidence.

Barbara Johnson

One night, Bill and I were listening to an African-American pastor on the radio encouraging his congregation. With a heartfelt genuine compassion for his people, he kept repeating Psalm 30:5. "Weeping endures for the night!" he would say. "But joy comes in the morning! Let me hear you, now. Weeping endures for the night ..." The people would sing that phrase back to him.

"But joy comes in the morning!" With one great voice, they returned the affirmation: "Joy comes in the morning!"

As we listened, the problems in our own lives seemed to settle into perspective in the immense power of God and his great faithfulness.

No matter how tragic the circumstances seem, no matter how long the spiritual drought, no matter how long and dark the days, the dawn will come. We will know that our God has been there all along. We will hear him say, through it all, "Hold on, my child, joy comes in the morning!"

Gloria Gaither

*Because of the LORD's great love we
are not consumed,
for his compassions never fail.
They are new every morning;
great is your faithfulness.*
Lamentations 3:22–23

The LORD is faithful, and he will
strengthen and protect you from
the evil one.

2 Thessalonians 3:3

He who began a good work in you will carry
it on to completion until the day of Christ
Jesus.

Philippians 1:6

*Your love, O LORD, reaches to the heavens,
your faithfulness to the skies.*
Psalm 36:5

Catastrophe or Happy Ending?

We need to recognize the vast difference between mere inconvenience and a major catastrophe. Nobody ever said life is easy, trouble-free, or without problems. Everyone knows that. The secret to handling problems is how we view them. It's an attitude thing. Running out of coffee is inconvenient. A rained-out picnic is inconvenient. But a smashed jaw, broken cheekbone, crushed nose, and missing eye? We're talking catastrophe!

Maybe I'm just a cockeyed optimist, but I think life is to be experienced joyfully rather than endured grudgingly. We know it brings complexities and trouble. Scripture affirms that. But why do we take minor irritations so seriously? Why do we act as though it's the end of the world? Think of the pain and conflict we would spare ourselves, the stress we would forego, if we just realized mere inconveniences can be survived.

Luci Swindoll

believe the world is shaped by the hand of a loving God. The Bible shows that we are an Easter people living in a Good Friday world, not Good Friday people living in an Easter world. That means we are destined for joy no matter how difficult our daily life. Something in us responds to the happiness other people experience, because we glimpse life as God intends it to be! It is an image imprinted in the spirit of Easter morning—pure, powerful, and potent, like the resurrection.

So go out there and help create all the happy endings you can. Don't be afraid of tears—your own or those of neighbors, family, friends, or strangers. You will have your share of Good Fridays, but Easter will come. Remember, moist eyes are good. Trembling lips are acceptable. Quivering voices won't hurt anybody. Though tears may disorient some people or send others running for cover, they are signals there is something deeper to be understood.

Go ahead and let the tears flow. But know, too, that the blue of heaven is far bigger than gray clouds beneath.

Barbara Johnson

Promises for Catastrophes and Happy Endings

Do not fear, for I am with you;
    do not be dismayed, for I am your God.
I will strengthen you and help you;
    I will uphold you with my righteous
        right hand.
                    Isaiah 41:10

No temptation has seized you except what is common to man. And God is faithful; he will not let you be tempted beyond what you can bear. But when you are tempted, he will also provide a way out so that you can stand up under it.
        1 Corinthians 10:13

Let us acknowledge the LORD;
    let us press on to acknowledge him.
As surely as the sun rises,
    he will appear;
he will come to us like the winter rains,
    like the spring rains that water the earth.
        Hosea 6:3

The Blessing of Courage

Whenever I find myself feeling weary and overwhelmed by the commitments I've made to my family, friends, publishers, and the Women of Faith tour, I remember Jesus' words: "From everyone who has been given much, much will be demanded; and from the one who has been entrusted with much, much more will be asked" (Luke 12:48).

Many blessings have been given to me. I know God didn't bless me with these gifts so I could sit back in the recliner and keep them all to myself.

Sometimes life becomes so complicated we feel as if we've gone as far as we can down this stressful highway. We imagine ourselves smashed up against a brick wall, unable to answer one more call, hear one more complaint, or even take one more breath. When that's the image that fills your mind, change the brick wall to God. Imagine yourself pressed tightly against his heart, wrapped in his everlasting arms, soothed by his life-giving breath. Picture yourself encircled in God's love, soaked in his strength. Then step out onto the highway once more.

Barbara Johnson

Courage and fear. Those two attributes are strange bedmates. It would seem impossible to experience both of them at the same time; yet I believe that's the challenge of the Christian life. Fear tells us that life is unpredictable, anything can happen, but courage replies quietly, "Yes, but God is in control."

If we will stop for a moment during our cluttered lives to reflect, we will realize this life is not a rehearsal. This is it. How will we choose to live?

I want to live a passionate life. I want to live a life that recognizes the fears but moves out with courage. I want to show the world the eternal mystery of what God can do through a miserable sinner sold out to him. Why would I settle for anything less? Life is tough, but God is faithful.

Sheila Walsh

Have I not commanded you? Be strong and courageous. Do not be terrified; do not be discouraged, for the LORD your God will be with you wherever you go.
Joshua 1:9

The LORD says: "Fear not, for I have redeemed you;
I have summoned you by name;
you are mine."
Isaiah 43:1

He gives strength to the weary
and increases the power of the weak.
Even youths grow tired and weary,
and young men stumble and fall;
but those who hope in the LORD
will renew their strength.
They will soar on wings like eagles;
they will run and not grow weary,
they will walk and not be faint.
Isaiah 40:29–31

God did not give us a spirit of timidity, but a spirit of power, of love and of self-discipline.
2 Timothy 1:7

Trusting Through the Tears

God washes us and cleans us up. His love rinses away the residue we pick up trying to protect ourselves from life's scratchy circumstances. When he is finished with us, we are shining, transparent, and lustrous.

Certainly the rain falls on the just and the unjust (chiefly on the just, because the unjust steal their umbrellas). But a few splashes of pain don't get me down for long. In the cesspools of life, I remember the colorful splashes of joy. I take my rainbow with me and share it with others!

We cannot protect ourselves from trouble, but we can dance through the puddles of life with a rainbow smile, twirling the only umbrella we need—the umbrella of God's love. His covering of grace is sufficient for any problem we may have.

Barbara Johnson

No matter who you are, you are made in God's image. Your life has eternal significance through Christ. Even in the most stable relationships, at times we can't be there for each other. But Christ will always be there. Christ is with you today as he was yesterday and will be tomorrow, and when you lay your head down for the last time, your life will be just beginning.

Where do you find yourself today? Perhaps you are worried about a child who has wandered away from God, and fear grips your heart for him or her. Perhaps you look at a pile of bills and a fragile balance in your checkbook, and fear squeezes tight.

How can you trust? I encourage you to take a leap into the arms of the One who is able to fill your heart with love and throw your fears to the wind. Christ did not come to remove all our troubles but to walk with us through every one of them. So, take a leap. Take a flying leap!

Sheila Walsh

Promises About Trusting Through Tears

You will keep in perfect peace
him whose mind is steadfast,
because he trusts in you.
Trust in the LORD forever,
for the LORD, the LORD, is the Rock
eternal.
Isaiah 26:3–4

Trust in the LORD with all your
heart
and lean not on your own
understanding;
in all your ways acknowledge
him,
and he will make your paths
straight.
Proverbs 3:5–6

Those who trust in the LORD are
like Mount Zion,
which cannot be shaken
but endures forever.
Psalm 125:1

The Joy Buster of Fear

I have envisioned certain fears that I kept trying to keep ahead of, only to find that when I stopped and faced them, there really was nothing to fear after all. What I needed to do was quit trying to avoid them and face them instead.

After my husband died, I didn't think I could handle money matters like taxes, interest rates, and investments. I had no choice but to turn and face that fear. I would still rather deal with investments like broccoli, cauliflower, and grapefruit, but I have learned it won't leave me dead on the beach to read a tax form.

Facing fears with a prayer on my lips and faith in my heart allows me not only to trust God more but also to experience victory that comes from no one but him. Actually, that is a rather exhilarating way to stay fit.

Marilyn Meberg

Sometimes, despite our best intentions, we find ourselves wandering in a wilderness of anxiety, lost and unable to find our way out. I know. For years I felt that way. Nothing seemed to work; I felt stripped and anxious, unable to determine what my mission in life should be.

I didn't know how to set my sights on God and let him lead me where to go.

It's true that goals help us to be disciplined and to aim our energies toward accomplishing what we've set out to do. So goals in and of themselves aren't bad. But for me, setting goals and not leaning on God had led me into a perplexing and fretful place. I learned that first I needed to humbly go before God and give him my concerns. Then he would provide me with direction.

You may be in the same wilderness I was, anxiously wandering around, feeling aimless and without a map, fearful that disaster is headed straight toward you. Relinquish your anxieties to God for he cares for you. Direction will come in God's good time.

Thelma Wells

Primises About Overcoming Fear

Jesus immediately said to them: "Take courage! It is I. Don't be afraid."
Matthew 14:27

Jesus said, "Peace I leave with you; my peace I give you. I do not give to you as the world gives. Do not let your hearts be troubled and do not be afraid."
John 14:27

Do not fear what they fear; do not be frightened. But in your hearts set apart Christ as LORD.
1 Peter 3:14–15

*Do not fear, for I am with you;
do not be dismayed, for I am your God.
I will strengthen you and help you;
I will uphold you with my righteous
right hand.*
Isaiah 41:10

*He who dwells in the shelter of the Most
        High
    will rest in the shadow of the Almighty.
I will say of the LORD, "He is my refuge and
        my fortress,
    my God, in whom I trust."
If you make the Most High your dwelling—
    even the LORD, who is my refuge—
then no harm will befall you,
    no disaster will come near your tent.
For he will command his
        angels concerning you
    to guard you in all your ways;
they will lift you up in their hands,
    so that you will not strike
        your foot against a stone.
You will tread upon the lion and the cobra;
    you will trample the great
        lion and the serpent.
"Because he loves me," says the LORD, "I
        will rescue him;
    I will protect him, for he
        acknowledges my name.
He will call upon me, and I will answer
        him;
    I will be with him in trouble,
    I will deliver him and honor him.
With long life will I satisfy him
    and show him my salvation."*
                Psalm 91:1–2; 9–16

Give Joy a Boost

The Boost of a Joyful Outlook

I've decided to get into a good humor and stay that way. That's why I want to treat people with kindness and give them a smile wherever I meet them, regardless of how they treat me. The smile, the kindness, comes back.

Let your joy out. One way I do that is to give people something to laugh about. How? I collect jokes and write down everything that I hear that makes me brighten up. I make amusement a ministry because chuckles are better than a therapist. They are aloe vera for the sunburns of life. When the dumps take their toll, laughter provides the exact change to get you through.

Whatever your troubles, try looking at them by the light of a different star. Go ahead; don't be afraid. Find a wacky angle, a new twist. Offer trouble a little serious thought, then turn it upside down and look at it through God-colored glasses. Chew on trouble's possibilities for making you smarter, better, stronger, kinder. Then take the curved weapon I call joy and toss trouble by its funny side out into the world.

Barbara Johnson

I wasn't all that thrilled about flying. If the good LORD had meant for us to be up in the air, he would have required us to live in hangars instead of homes.

Yet one day I realized navigating the airways was to be a constant part of my life, and I was going to lose my joy a lot if I didn't make some altitude adjustments. I needed another perspective. So I'll put on a gratitude attitude before boarding because:

1.   It provides a way to travel that allows me to dart about the country and do things I could never do otherwise.

2.   I might be able to offer a word of kindness to an anxious traveler or a stressed flight attendant.

3.   As unskilled at cooking as I am, I can still offer up a better meal than the airlines!

Maybe you find yourself taxiing around your home or office with a jet-sized 'tude. Try sitting still and ask the LORD for a fresh perspective for an old routine. Then prepare for takeoff and enjoy the amazing view.

Patsy Clairmont

Promises for a Joyful Outlook

Everyone born of God overcomes the world.
1 John 5:4

The one who is in you is greater than the one who is in the world.
1 John 4:4

In all their distress he too was
        distressed,
    and the angel of his
        presence saved them.
In his love and mercy he
    redeemed them;
    he lifted them up and
        carried them
    all the days of old.
            Isaiah 63:9

Whoever touches you touches the apple of God's eye.
Zechariah 2:8

A Second Look Yields Forgiveness

Have you heard of International Forgiveness Week? Sure enough, I found it on the calendar, smack-dab in the middle of winter. In winter you feel dull and drab and closed in, as though spring will never come. You are restless, cold, and irritable, just the way you feel when you hold a grudge.

Forgiveness enables you to bury your grudge in the icy earth and put the past behind you. You flush resentment away by being the first to forgive. Forgiveness fashions your future. It is a brave and brash thing to do. The gutsiest decision you can make. As you forgive others, winter will soon make way for springtime as fresh joy pushes up through the soil of your heart.

Forgiveness is a stunning principle, your ticket out of hate and fear and chaos. I know what regret feels like; I've earned my credentials. But I also know what forgiveness feels like, because God has so graciously forgiven me. Forgiveness frees you of the past so you can make good choices today. Look to Jesus as your example.

Barbara Johnson

I walked into a Dallas bank to meet with an executive vice president about customer-service training. I went up to the secretary's desk, smiled, and announced my name and my reason for being there. The secretary stopped working, looked me up and down, gave me no response, stood up, and walked off, leaving me standing there. She had decided I wasn't worth a nod, let alone a smile or a handshake.

When I taught the customer-service class, she was a top participant. She was pleasant, positive, polite, and poised. But none of that held any meaning for me. Her lasting impression remained my first impression of her.

But I wasn't following Christ's admonition to give people room to make a second impression. I needed to give her a second chance.

Maybe you have written a person off as someone you want nothing to do with. That person just might deserve a second chance.

God knows us inside out and outside in. He understands what motivates us and accepts us even in our worst moments. I want to be able to do the same for others.

Thelma Wells

Promises About Forgiveness

In him we have redemption through his blood, the forgiveness of sins, in accordance with the riches of God's grace.

Ephesians 1:7

He has rescued us from the dominion of darkness and brought us into the kingdom of the Son he loves, in whom we have redemption, the forgiveness of sins.

Colossians 1:13–14

The LORD our God is merciful and forgiving, even though we have rebelled against him.

Daniel 9:9

Be kind and compassionate to one another, forgiving each other, just as in Christ God forgave you.

Ephesians 4:32

Walking with a Gratitude Attitude

God is at work in all of life, if we will only see his hand and listen and learn. God is talking to us all the time. We imagine that if good things happen, then God loves us, and if life seems difficult, then he doesn't. This isn't true. Join hands with God in your life. Throw open the doors and let the sun come pouring in. God is at work! God is at work! God is at work! God's grace shows up to plug our leaky lives. That's the gospel. That's the good news.

Do you really want to find joy? Then reach out. Pure joy learns to take one day—one hour—at a time. Throw yourself on God's mercy. Ask him to show you his love. Give him some room to move in. The gift is yours. Ask God here and now to allow you a glimpse of his love.

Let God love you, and even before you "feel" the warmth, start walking a thank-you journey.

Sheila Walsh

Harvest time in Indiana. The wide plows turn the traces of cornstalks and dry soybean plants under, leaving the fresh black earth like a velvet carpet laid in neat squares. The squirrels skitter around the yard, stuffing acorns and walnuts in their jaws, racing off to bury their treasure.

This is the season to finish things, to tie up loose ends, to save and store, to harvest and be sure there is enough of everything that matters to last us through the hard times.

And how does one finish a season of the heart? How can we harvest and store the bounty of the spirit and save the fruits we cannot see? Gratitude is the instrument of harvest. It ties the golden sheaves in bundles; it plucks the swollen kernels in great bales.

Thank God for harvest time, a time for finishing what's been started, a time to be aware, to take account, and to realize the life we've been given.

God has promised that if we harvest well with the tools of thanksgiving, there will be seeds for planting in the spring.

Gloria Gaither

Promises for a Gratitude Attitude

Speak to one another with psalms, hymns and spiritual songs. Sing and make music in your heart to the LORD, always giving thanks to God the Father for everything, in the name of our LORD Jesus Christ.

Ephesians 5:19–20

Know that the LORD is God.
It is he who made us, and we are his;
we are his people, the sheep of his pasture.
Enter his gates with thanksgiving and his courts with praise;
give thanks to him and praise his name.

Psalm 100:3–4

Whatever you do, whether in word or deed, do it all in the name of the LORD Jesus, giving thanks to God the Father through him.

Colossians 3:17

The Joy of Aging

Television journalist Dan Rather once asked a 106-year-old man to disclose his secret of long life. The old man rocked back and forth in his chair before answering. Finally he replied, "Keep breathing."

Sure, growing older is stressful, but using your funny bone to subdue that kind of stress works wonders! When you hear snap, crackle, pop, and it isn't your cereal, don't panic. Laughter defuses insults, soothes aching muscles, and counteracts the humiliation of what is happening to your body and mind.

Gerontologist Ann E. Gerike says we can develop a new way of thinking about our physical limitations as we age. After a lifetime of straining to be "the perfect perky ideal," finally your breasts can relax. And that extra weight around the middle (hence the term *middle age?*)—it's just cuddlier body lines! So as birthdays come, don't think of yourself as growing old; you've just reached that vibrant metallic age: silver in your hair, gold in your teeth, and lead in your bottom!

Barbara Johnson

I feel encased within a timepiece that can at times rob me of my peace. Left unto ourselves, some of us would race, and others of us would rust. Either way, we would speed past or sleep through the joy. We need to make peace with the timepiece so we don't spend our time beating our heads against the clock.

Here are some tips. I'll try them if you will.

1. Don't cram every day so full you can't enjoy the journey.

2. Don't under plan and miss the thrill of a fruitful day.

3. Don't underestimate a nap, a rocking chair, and a good book.

4. Don't become a sloth.

5. Do offer your gratitude for the moments assigned to you.

6. Do celebrate even the passing of days.

Patsy Clairmont

Promises About Aging

Your beauty should not come from outward adornment, such as braided hair and the wearing of gold jewelry and fine clothes. Instead, it should be that of your inner self, the unfading beauty of a gentle and quiet spirit, which is of great worth in God's sight.
1 Peter 3:3–4

*Even to your old age and gray
        hairs
    I am he, I am he who will
        sustain you.
I have made you and I will
        carry you;
    I will sustain you and I will
        rescue you.*
Isaiah 46:4

*Gray hair is a crown of splendor;
    it is attained by a righteous life.*
Proverbs 16:31

*Age should speak;
    advanced years should teach wisdom.*
Job 32:7

The Joy Buster of Worry

Dear LORD, like a child with her mom,
when I say now, I mean *right now*! Thank
you for not always dropping everything in the
universe and rushing to my rescue. Instead,
you have allowed me to feel my neediness and
experience my limitations so I will understand
that it is you who will (eventually) save me. I
don't want to refuse your perfect plan; I want
to find refuge in you. Then I will have the
stamina to make it to the end. Amen."

Patsy Clairmont

I have a bit of a "germ thing;" and I don't like cafeterias. So I was eating my entire meal [at a cafeteria] with an oversized spoon I had found in an obscure container slightly behind the soft ice-cream machine.

"How long have you had this germ thing?" Luci asked.

"Since the sixth grade," I replied. "Our science teacher had us all touch some specially treated sponge, and overnight it grew bacteria cultures that we watched develop into various colorful and horrifying configurations. I've never been the same since."

Luci slowly put down her fork and studied it for a second. Then, with renewed enthusiasm, she announced, "If those germs haven't gotten me by this time in my life, I don't think they ever will!"

Her healthy response reminded me that for me to fear the unseen and to worry about its potential to do me harm throttles my joy. Of course, one should observe hygienic health practices, but if carried to an extreme, they can lead to wrestling with a too-large spoon in a cafeteria with plenty of right-sized forks.

Marilyn Meberg

Promises About Freedom from Worry

*Cast your cares on the LORD
and he will sustain you;
he will never let the righteous
fall.*
Psalm 55:22

Jesus said, "Look at the birds of the air; they do not sow or reap or store away in barns, and yet your heavenly Father feeds them. Are you not much more valuable than they? Who of you by worrying can add a single hour to his life? And why do you worry about clothes? See how the lilies of the field grow. They do not labor or spin. Yet I tell you that not even Solomon in all his splendor was dressed like one of these. If that is how God clothes the grass of the field, which is here today and tomorrow is thrown into the fire, will he not much more clothe you, O you of little faith? So do not worry, saying, 'What shall we eat?' or 'What shall we drink?' or 'What shall we wear?' ... But seek first his kingdom and his righteousness, and all these things will be given to you as well. Therefore do not worry about tomorrow, for tomorrow will worry about itself."

Matthew 6:26–34

A Respite from Our Tasks

Mmmm ... So good to get away from the everyday of life. Perfect solitude. Time to reflect, read, write, and pray.

God has manifested himself in breathtaking sunsets and a dancing porpoise show. "Together now, up and out of the water. Smile and dive," say the porpoise. "Under the boat and out. Higher this time. They love us!"

Today we saw a rainbow—a complete rainbow. We considered sailing off to find the pot of gold. But whatever would we do with a pot of gold? And who would believe our story?

Tonight we made up silly songs and poetry, even a joint-venturing one about the captain of our ship. We were silly beyond words.

And to think we almost didn't come. "Too busy," we said. Busy doing what? It slips my mind just now.

Sue Buchanan

As a child raised in rural communities with few libraries, I was thrilled when the bookmobile rolled into my area every other week. With my books strapped to the back carrier of my bike, I would eagerly pedal a little more than a mile to where the bookmobile was parked. Happily fortified with new reading selections, I'd pedal back home, clamber up the makeshift ladder to my treehouse, and settle in.

When was the last time you settled in for a mindlessly pleasant read? Why don't you do that more often? What's continually driving you to be productive?

Perhaps some of you, like me, are missing out on recreational activity that has no purpose other than to give a needed respite from our task-oriented lives. Wouldn't it be fun occasionally to produce nothing, accomplish nothing, and contribute to nothing? Maybe that means reading a book that doesn't require a pen; maybe it's a cup of something at a coffee house; or maybe it's a meander through the mall or a stroll (not a jog) through the park. The possibilities for nothing are endless.

Marilyn Meberg

Promises About a Respite from Our Tasks

Jesus said, "Come to me, all you who are weary and burdened, and I will give you rest. Take my yoke upon you and learn from me, for I am gentle and humble in heart, and you will find rest for your souls."

Matthew 11:28–29

Be at rest once more, O my soul, for the LORD has been good to you.

Psalm 116:7

There remains, then, a Sabbath-rest for the people of God; for anyone who enters God's rest also rests from his own work, just as God did from his. Let us, therefore, make every effort to enter that rest.

Hebrews 4:9–11

Stop, Look, & Sniff

Two young children were playing a bedtime game they called "God is ..." They took turns finishing the sentence with positive descriptions of God. Six-year-old Missy finally ventured, "God smells good all the time."

"That's dumb," her older brother said.

But Missy insisted. "Sometimes he smells like orange blossoms and sometimes like apples. Tonight he smells like strawberries."

Maybe Missy was really just enjoying the smell of the strawberry bubble bath that was hardly dry on her skin. But maybe Missy can lead us to a new appreciation of a spiritual metaphor. In 2 Corinthians 2:15, Paul says that we believers are "the aroma of Christ."

God wants to use you to spread the aroma of Christ. Are you able to take joy in that metaphor? Can you inhale a little deeper and longer to enjoy the fragrance yourself?

Stop the rat race. Enjoy the rich aromas in your life—the ones God gives in nature and the ones God gives through the witness of human kindness. Stop and enjoy the sights, tastes, and smells of God's good gifts.

Sheila Walsh

It is often in the small things—the ordinary moments turned extraordinary—that I recognize his presence and can sense his kindness and tenderness.

My friend Allyson's baby, Logan, seems to have an inner joy that comes straight from heaven. One day as Allyson and I were running errands, she left me in the car with him. Every time I turned to look at him, he would giggle with such zeal that I wondered whether he could catch his breath. Any sadness I felt that day was washed away as I listened to Logan laugh.

Once, hurrying through a busy airport to get to my gate on time for a connecting flight, I came upon a lady in a wheelchair. Amid the chaos of the hundreds of people rushing around us, my eyes met hers. The sweetest smile appeared on her face. I smiled back, but I knew she would never fully realize how that small gesture had filled my soul.

I believe that God is in our everyday. Many moments occur in our lives that reveal his face, his touch, his voice. Look for him today. He will be found.

Kathy Troccoli

Promises About Stopping and Looking

This is the day the LORD has made;
let us rejoice and be glad in it.
Psalm 118:24

Taste and see that the LORD is good;
blessed is the man who takes
refuge in him.
Psalm 34:8

A cheerful look brings joy to
the heart,
and good news gives health
to the bones.
Proverbs 15:30

Light is sweet,
and it pleases the eyes to see the sun.
Ecclesiastes 11:7

We are to God the aroma of Christ among
those who are being saved and those who are
perishing.
2 Corinthians 2:15

A Green Thumb of Beauty

Gardening fever is upon us. It seems as though everyone is a gardener, even if they live in a big-city apartment. Even if they have eleven green thumbs. Even if they wouldn't pull weeds for a million dollars. Even if they don't know the difference between a spade and a rake. Even if they hate vegetables and bugs, are allergic to bees, or have spring hayfever. Suddenly everyone is a gardening maniac.

Well, there are certain things anybody can plant—sweet P's in a straight row, for instance: prayer, patience, peace, passion. But it's not enough for a gardener to love flowers. A gardener also must hate weeds. As good plants grow, you must pinch off bitter ones like panic, paranoia, and passivity. And by the way, while gardening, do squash pride. And please, lettuce love one another at all times.

Begin now to cultivate your half-acre of love. All it takes is a few seeds no larger than grains of sand. The blossom of a good deed fades with time, but that lasting perfume is the joy you receive from doing it.

Barbara Johnson

I was driving down a familiar road in Nashville one fall day when I almost drove off the road, the beauty was so intense. It looked as if God had sent in a team of the world's finest artists overnight, and I was privy to the opening day of his spectacle.

The show was a sight to behold. Every tree had changed to shades of deepest gold and robin red, to sun-kissed yellow and pumpkin orange. Leaves danced in the air and brushed against my windshield.

Notice the colors in your world! Look around your own home. How can you add a touch of beauty? Every one of us can do one small thing to add beauty to our workplace or kitchen or bedroom. File the papers cluttering the desk. Re-cover a pillow. Rearrange the furniture. Light a candle on the table.

Maybe it's time for a new hairstyle or makeover. The makeup counters at the mall will give you a complimentary makeover with no obligation to buy. A friend tells me there's nothing like a professional shoeshine for lifting up a bad day. Open your eyes. Brighten your world.

Sheila Walsh

Promises About Beauty

He has made everything beautiful in its time.
Ecclesiastes 3:11

*Charm is deceptive, and beauty
    is fleeting;
but a woman who fears the
    LORD is to be praised.
Proverbs 31:30*

Your beauty should not come from outward
adornment, such as braided hair and the
wearing of gold jewelry and fine clothes.
Instead, it should be that of your inner self,
the unfading beauty of a gentle and quiet
spirit, which is of great worth in God's sight.
For this is the way the holy women of the past
who put their hope in God used to make
themselves beautiful.
    1 Peter 3:3–5

The Joy of Enjoying Life

God can use you even when you're living between estrogen and death. Age on, girls, the best is yet to be! Remember that each day is like a suitcase—every person gets the same size, but some people figure out how to pack more into theirs.

Life is short. Each year passes more quickly than the previous one. It's easy to deny yourself many of life's simple pleasures because you want to be practical. Forget about practical and decide instead to become a joy collector. Always be on the lookout for gifts without ribbons. God is strewing them across your path right now. His gifts come tagged with a note: "Life can be wonderful. Do your best not to miss it!" Enjoy what is before it isn't anymore.

God will scatter surprise blessings across your path in the next few years. Don't be like the woman who described herself as passive and bored, a "mush melon living in a middle-aged frame." Instead be zany and giddy. Dare to slip on a pair of bunny slippers once in a while! Surprise yourself! Enjoy the little things because one day you'll look back and realize they were the big things!

Barbara Johnson

Since I travel most weekends, Monday is the day I unpack. That's always a mess, with stuff everywhere and suitcases lying about.

Then there's the laundry ... piles of clothes that need washing. And those piles multiply! I have this theory that, after the LORD comes and time is no more, somewhere, in a corner of the world, dirty laundry will still be waiting.

On Monday I must make stops at the grocery store, the cleaners, the bank, the post office, the service station, the hairdresser. Mondays annoy me.

But in another way, I love Mondays. I love unloading all my stuff out of the suitcase and organizing it back where it belongs. I love pulling fresh laundry from the dryer and folding it while it's still warm.

On Monday nights, I feel genuine joy, having such a sense of accomplishment. So what's the difference? Why do I sometimes get bogged down with chores, hating the day? Then, at other times, I get fired up with enthusiasm, loving the day? Perspective! Perspective is everything. The busiest days can become our most joyful.

Luci Swindoll

All the days ordained for me
were written in your book
before one of them came to be.
Psalm 139:16

It is God who arms me with strength
and makes my way perfect.
He makes my feet like the feet of a
deer;
he enables me to stand on
the heights.
Psalm 18:32–33

Go, eat your food with gladness, and drink your wine with a joyful heart, for it is now that God favors what you do.

Ecclesiastes 9:7

That everyone may eat and drink, and find satisfaction in all his toil—this is the gift of God.

Ecclesiastes 3:13

The Joy of Following God's Direction

My experience with the prompting of the Holy Spirit has been that when he directs you, there is an indescribable peace in your body, mind, and spirit that you feel but can't explain to anyone who hasn't experienced it. God's Spirit would never direct us to do anything contrary to Scripture, so we have a guidebook that can help us, too.

You've probably said in certain situations, "I knew in my heart that such and such was ..." Those are probably times God's Spirit was prompting you.

I need to be responsive to the Holy Spirit. I have found him to be the greatest organizer, time manager, administrator, and scheduler.

What will you do when you think you're being prompted by the Holy Spirit to take a certain action? I'd suggest you ask for clarity. Wait for the answer. I can't tell you how you will know when the answer comes, but I can tell you that you will experience peace in your mind, body, and soul that you can't describe. Listen to your heart.

Thelma Wells

Vision is when you see it and others don't. Faith is when you do it and others won't. With vision and faith, things can be done.

One of the greatest by products of believing in something and then going for it is joy. I've often said, "My favorite thing in life is doing something new while having a good time." That's the essence of joy.

Let's get practical. Perhaps you have an idea of something you would like to do, but you're scared. You've never done anything like it before. Maybe the idea just won't go away. But it's outside your comfort zone, and you don't feel adequate for the task. Start to pray, *LORD, if this desire is from you, will you bring it to pass? Help me know where to start.*

And then start. This is the faith part. Work hard. Do what makes sense to you. Ask the LORD whom to talk to who might help you. Talk with them.

What has he given you the desire to do? You can do it.

Luci Swindoll

Promises About God's Direction

*In your unfailing love you will lead
    the people you have redeemed.
In your strength you will guide them
    to your holy dwelling.*
        Exodus 15:13

*Teach me to do your will,
    for you are my God;
may your good Spirit
    lead me on level ground.*
        Psalm 143:10

If you are pleased with me, teach me
your ways so I may know you and
continue to find favor with you.
    Exodus 33:13

*Good and upright is the LORD;
    therefore he instructs sinners in his
        ways.
He guides the humble in what is right
    and teaches them his way.*
        Psalm 25:8–9

Remembering and Being Remembered

At the call center in Denver International Airport, each of the thirty-six operators may answer as many as 260 calls per day. Then they relay messages to some of the ninety-thousand passengers and others that pass through the concourses within any twenty-four-hour period.

Sometimes the messages are frantic, such as one from a daughter who helped her father carry his luggage to the check-in counter for his trip to Bangkok and then returned to the parking lot to discover a major problem. That's when the call center might relay a message begging, "Don't get on that plane! You have Sarah's only set of car keys in your pocket."

When I read about these relayed messages, I chuckled, but then I thought of how fortunate we are that when we need to get an urgent message to our Father in heaven, we don't have to route our plea through a busy call center. Isaiah 58:9 promises, "Then you will call, and the LORD will answer."

Barbara Johnson

Remembering is important to God. He encourages us to make memories. In Joshua 3–4, we read the account of the Israelites moving the ark of the covenant across the flooded Jordan River. After the water parted to allow the ark and the Israelites to cross, God commanded the leaders of the twelve tribes to take one stone each from the river and to place it where the priests had stood with the ark when they arrived safely on the other shore. "These stones are to be a memorial to the people of Israel forever" (Joshua 4:7). They are still there today.

We're encouraged to remember days of old, the wonders of God, the Sabbath, God's deeds and our struggles, our Creator, our youth, and that life is short.

If you've not yet begun to create memories, start now. Load up your camera with film, fill that pen with ink, and capture the miracles and wonders that come your way.

Surround yourself with whatever it takes to be reminded. God is faithful. Don't ever forget that.

Luci Swindoll

Promises About Remembering

The eyes of the LORD are on the righteous
and his ears are attentive to their cry.
Psalm 34:15

Before they call I will answer;
while they are still speaking I will hear.
Isaiah 65:24

You will call upon me and come and pray to
me, and I will listen to you. You will seek me
and find me when you seek me with all your
heart.

Jeremiah 29:12–13

Only be careful, and watch
yourselves closely so that you do
not forget the things your eyes have
seen or let them slip from your heart
as long as you live.
Deuteronomy 4:9

The Joy of Thankfulness

I don't know about you, but I don't want to live my life in the past lane. I want to find a zillion things to be thankful for today. One little girl was overjoyed one Thanksgiving Day because broccoli wasn't on the table! When God does make broccoli part of the menu, I've learned it's only because he has a greater good in mind.

What are you thankful for right this moment? Start today by being grateful for the tiniest things: water to drink, a moment to rest, the color of a flower or sunset or bird. A piece of bread. A song on the radio. Keep looking for sights, smells, sounds that make you feel pleasure. Write them down.

Let's decide to be thankful and encourage one another to cultivate grateful hearts. God is thankful for you. He gave his Son to reclaim your life. He invites you into the joy of salvation. That's an awful lot to be thankful for right there. And something else to be thankful for? The fact that you are here to be thankful!

Barbara Johnson

Let's be thankful! Thankful for plenty—plenty and more—of things to eat and wear; of shelter and warmth; of beauty. Plenty of things that money can't buy, such as tenderness and inspiration and revelation and insight.

Thankful for health—health that we take so for granted that we schedule our lives, assuming always that everything will be normal.

Thankful for family—family with individual personalities, gifts, needs, and dreams, each such a gift—all feeding into what we are and what we will become.

Thankful for friends—for stimulating, vivacious, provoking, comforting, disturbing, encouraging, agitating, blessing, loving, warming, forgiving friends.

And thankful for the courage to go on trusting people, risking love, daring to believe in what could be, all because of the confirming experience of daily trusting God and finding him utterly trustworthy.

Gloria Gaither

Promises About Being Thankful

Just as you received Christ Jesus as LORD, continue to live in him, rooted and built up in him, strengthened in the faith as you were taught, and overflowing with thankfulness.
Colossians 2:6–7

Sing and make music in your heart to the LORD, always giving thanks to God the Father for everything.
Ephesians 5:19–20

Whatever you do, whether in word or deed, do it all in the name of the LORD Jesus, giving thanks to God the Father through him.
Colossians 3:17

Through Jesus, therefore, let us continually offer to God a sacrifice of praise.
Hebrews 13:15

The Seven Deadly Joy Busters

As believers in God, there are places where we should definitely not, under any circumstances, even think of parking.

Do not park by life's defeats. Where has life gotten you down? Don't park there! Move on.

Do not park at anger. Storing up hostility will only boomerang on you in the long run.

Do not park at escape. There is no good time for quitting. Don't give up— get going!

Do not park at discouragement. Optimism actually promotes physical as well as emotional healing.

Do not park at worry. Think on what is right and true and lovely (Philippians 4:8). Who knows what possibilities are just around the corner?

Do not park at guilt. Move on by receiving Jesus as your Savior, accepting God's forgiveness, and freely forgiving others. Put the past behind you. Begin again. Learn all you can from your mistakes, and with God's help, make a U-turn at each one.

Barbara Johnson

A saboteur of joy is the many ways we are disappointed with ourselves. We live with regrets that drag us down to the depths, sometimes to the depths of despair.

Many of us who have been Christians for years do not perceive ourselves as sinners of the first degree. We get up every morning intending to serve and please God, and yet, with the apostle Paul, we do what we don't want to do. We miss the mark and then live in regret.

I think of the apostle Paul—a Christian—admitting his own weakness: "What a wretched man I am! Who will rescue me from this body of death?" That question is followed by an exclamation: "Thanks be to God—through Jesus Christ our LORD!" (Romans 7:24–25). Jesus is the only one who could rescue me from myself.

God knows about the secret abortion, the private fantasy life, the hatred you hold in your heart. It is only when we confess these things to God that he can fill the broken, empty places with his joy.

Sheila Walsh

Promises About Overcoming Deadly Joy Busters

There is now no condemnation for those who are in Christ Jesus.
Romans 8:1

I say to myself, "The LORD is my portion;
*   therefore I will wait for him."*
The LORD is good to those whose hope is
*   in him,*
*   to the one who seeks him;*
it is good to wait quietly
*   for the salvation of the LORD.*
Lamentations 3:24–26

Jesus said, "Do not worry about your life, what you will eat or drink; or about your body, what you will wear. Is not life more important than food, and the body more important than clothes?"

Matthew 6:25

Guard the good deposit that was entrusted to you—guard it with the help of the Holy Spirit.
2 Timothy 1:14

The Joy of Godly
Relationships

I used to find it hard to forge deep friendships with other women. I felt such a need for approval and acceptance; yet I was afraid to let the real me be seen in case I wasn't enough. The higher I erected a façade of fear around myself, the more I needed approval, but the less I was available to receive it. Hiding behind that wall, I didn't realize how much effort it would take for someone to scale those heights to find the real, scared, and unsure me.

Finally, I figured out I was inadequate to create or maintain relationships. Fortunately, at the same time, I realized Christ is enough for all of us. His mercy helps us to see others mercifully, and his loving acceptance of us enables us to accept ourselves and others. With that as a beginning point, we can relax, be ourselves, and come out from behind the protective walls we've erected. Then we can connect with others who have discovered the joy of just being themselves—flawed and silly, but of worth because of Jesus.

Sheila Walsh

Loving and being loved—being connected, valued, befriended, cherished by another—is a compelling need that permeates the life of every human being on God's earth. Yet neither love nor friendship can be manipulated or prescribed. You can't choose an attractive candidate and merely follow your top-ten list of things to do to make love happen. So how then are such relationships to come about? Is there anything we can do to develop a bond of companionship that is intimate, fulfilling, and even joyful?

Jesus Christ created a model of love, as he did of friendship: Along with the reassuring "I have loved you even as the Father has loved me ... I have told you this so that your joy may be full," we hear from his heart the welcoming words, "I have called you friend." Mind-boggling!

We need not set out in search for a friend; rather, we must simply set out to be the friend Christ modeled—anticipating the needs of others, wearing ourselves out at giving. Jesus died doing it. The rewards are infinite and joyous!

Joy MacKenzie

Promises About Godly Relationships

If we walk in the light, as he is in the light, we have fellowship with one another, and the blood of Jesus, his Son, purifies us from all sin.
1 John 1:7

Jesus said, "Greater love has no one than this, that he lay down his life for his friends. You are my friends if you do what I command."
John 15:13–14

Jesus said, "I have called you friends, for everything that I learned from my Father I have made known to you."
John 15:15

After Job had prayed for his friends, the LORD made him prosperous again and gave him twice as much as he had before.
Job 42:10

The Joy of Receiving Advice

God warns us of danger. We listen and are careful. But then we slough off. Even when we see warning signs, we think we're smart enough and have our act together. We don't listen or pay attention. That's when we fall and fail.

Whether you're climbing mountains or think you have a firm grip on everything that's important to you, you would be wise to look to the LORD. Remain humble and aware that your footing could slip at any time—or you could feel those things that are so precious to you slip out of your life without warning. We're on the way to glory land, but we ain't there yet!

Thelma Wells

I had been invited for a horseback ride. My husband, Les, didn't think me wise to accept the invitation. Les wasn't worried about the trail paths so much as he was my tailbone being splattered on the roadway.

My husband's cautions rang in my ears as I headed out. The only challenge I had was my stirrups. They were a little too long for my short legs, and I felt like a toe dancer as I stretched to keep my feet in the stirrups.

About six minutes into the ride, my leg muscles began to scream, "Are you out of your mind?" Finally, with my legs stretched far beyond their designed reach and with a kink in my back the size of New Hampshire, I pleaded my cause with the staff. They compassionately headed for the stable. As I deboarded, my legs wobbled as I toddled my way to a bench. For three days afterwards, my back felt like the horse had ridden me.

Do you find it difficult to take good advice? To live within your limitations? To admit when you're wrong? Just remember, if you get a backache from carrying your horse, don't be surprised.

Patsy Clairmont

Promises About Receiving Advice

The way of a fool seems right to him,
but a wise man listens to advice.
Proverbs 12:15

Let the wise listen and add to
their learning,
and let the discerning get
guidance.
Proverbs 1:5

If you accept my words
and store up my commands within you,
turning your ear to wisdom
and applying your heart to
understanding,
and if you call out for insight
and cry aloud for understanding,
and if you look for it as for silver
and search for it as for hidden treasure,
then you will understand the fear of the
LORD
and find the knowledge of God.
For the LORD gives wisdom,
and from his mouth come
knowledge and understanding.
Proverbs 2:1–6

Think About Your Heart Attitude

Women have always been able to make do with what life hands them, to create an ordered universe in the midst of chaos and stress. Women have always been able to make something from nothing, stretching the stew, making the worn-out clothes or opportunities into something new, smiling and caressing in spite of their own inclinations to give in to tears and fatigue, mothering the world. Yet, while their hands were performing the task at hand, their minds were racing on. Assimilating. Analyzing. Philosophizing.

So much of men's thinking is applied directly to their work. The result of their thinking is output, income, product. But much of what women think about does not create tangible products. Instead, they ponder the meaning and quality of life. Such pondering may not result in consumable products, but it can produce great souls who ask why instead of merely what and how. Women, after all, are about the industry of the heart.

Gloria Gaither

I'm all for nostalgia, but it's hard to be nostalgic when you can't remember anything. At least memory loss helps me dispense with regret and guilt. I'm moving on, anticipating where I'm heading, open to today's answers to today's problems.

Some people pause to reminisce and then get stuck there. Nowadays I may be slowing down, but I am definitely not settling back. I keep trying, just as my first-grade teacher taught me to do. And if at first I do succeed, I'll try not to look astonished.

How will the LORD use your life this year? This month? This day? Is there one thing you can do to make life better for someone else? Can you warm the home of an elderly friend? Chill out so a teenager can open up to your love? Knock on the door of a lonely single mom? Invite a seven-year-old for lemonade? The possibilities are endless. God expects us to use our brains and figure out what we can do to make a difference. Find out where he's working and join his crew.

Barbara Johnson

Promises About Your Heart Attitude

May the God of hope fill you with all joy and peace as you trust in him, so that you may overflow with hope by the power of the Holy Spirit.

Romans 15:13

Jesus said, "Whoever finds his life will lose it, and whoever loses his life for my sake will find it."

Matthew 10:39

Since, then, you have been raised with Christ, set your hearts on things above, where Christ is seated at the right hand of God.

Colossians 3:1

Those who hope in the LORD
    will renew their strength.
They will soar on wings like eagles;
    they will run and not grow weary,
    they will walk and not be faint.

Isaiah 40:31

Share the Joy

The Joy of a Reassuring Word

Sometimes the very desire for action leads to the neglect of action. We're so busy searching for the perfect opportunity, the most effective method, the favorable moment, that we not only disqualify ourselves for the mission and miss the joy, but an urgent need is left unanswered.

I have often experienced the pull of an inner voice, urging me to call a friend who is in need. Invariably, I address that urge by checking my watch to see if the time is appropriate, or by mentally reprioritizing my schedule to accommodate a more convenient arrangement.

Born of genuine concern for my friend, my determination to provide the most propitious response thwarts the entire effort. The perfect moment never arrives; there is never a convenient time.

When my friend most needed simply to hear a reassuring voice, I wasn't available. I was busy rearranging God's schedule. Are you, too?

Joy MacKenzie

One woman went to her doctor to get the results of a checkup. The doctor said, "I have good news and bad news. Which do you want first?"

She answered, "The good news!"

The doctor said, "You have twenty-four hours to live."

"Good grief," exclaimed the woman. "That's the good news? Then what's the bad news?"

"The bad news," replied the doctor, "is that I was supposed to tell you yesterday."

Don't let your life speed out of control. Live intentionally. Slice the time from your schedule. Do something today that will last beyond your lifetime.

Commit yourself to being a hope bringer no matter what. Hope looks for the good in people, opens doors for people, discovers what can be done to help, lights a candle, does not yield to cynicism. Hope sets people free. Be grateful today for the hope you've been given and then find creative ways to pass it on to someone else.

Barbara Johnson

Promises for Sharing Reassuring Words

How beautiful on the mountains
    are the feet of those who bring good
      news.
Isaiah 52:7

A word aptly spoken
    is like apples of gold in settings of silver.
      Proverbs 25:11

Like cold water to a weary soul
    is good news from a distant land.
      Proverbs 25:25

The Spirit of the Sovereign LORD is on me,
    because the LORD has anointed me
      to preach good news to the poor.
He has sent me to bind up
    the brokenhearted,
    to proclaim freedom for the captives
    and release from darkness for the
      prisoners.
      Isaiah 61:1

The Joy of Sharing Your Witness

God draws people to himself. Each of us is his mouthpiece on earth. Whether we say just the right thing or can't think of anything that seems right, all we can do is open our mouths and trust God to use us. That doesn't mean we shouldn't be prepared to offer a reasoned explanation for our faith, but it does take the pressure off of us. We are the instruments, but God is the One who must make the music through us.

Have you tried to explain a spiritual principle to someone lately and sounded only sour notes? Have you been stymied about how to make clear that thing which seems so obvious to you? Remembering your role and God's role can help to comfort you if you've blown it. It may even give you the push you need to increase your knowledge so you can sound off more eloquently next time.

Thelma Wells

If we want to spread hope and joy, if we want people to know our LORD and Savior Jesus Christ, let's stop faking who we are. The only thing that's separating them from us is that we are forgiven. Our problems are no less tragic. Our lives no less complicated. Our burdens no less heavy. For all of us, life is mostly a struggle to keep our weight down and our spirits up. The difference is that Christians have Someone who will go the distance with them.

In your desire to share the gospel, you may be the only Jesus someone else will ever meet. Be real and involved with people. They may be closer to the kingdom of heaven than you think. A good rule of thumb is to keep your heart a little softer than your head!

It's in the darkest places, after all, that the grace of God shines most brightly. That is where people begin to see him. By our scars we are recognized as belonging to him.

Ask the Holy Spirit to help you be genuine in all your relationships. And allow God to answer the world's questions through your life.

Barbara Johnson

Promises About Sharing Your Witness

Then Jesus came to them and said, "All authority in heaven and on earth has been given to me. Therefore go and make disciples of all nations, baptizing them in the name of the Father and of the Son and of the Holy Spirit, and teaching them to obey everything I have commanded you. And surely I am with you always, to the very end of the age."
Matthew 28:18–20

Jesus said, "You will receive power when the Holy Spirit comes on you; and you will be my witnesses in Jerusalem, and in all Judea and Samaria, and to the ends of the earth."
Acts 1:8

All the ends of the earth will see the salvation of our God.
Isaiah 52:10

The Deep Calling of Friendship

One of the deepest callings of friendship is to weep with those who weep. As I write, in autumn, I watch the leaves falling off my favorite tree outside my window. And so there are seasons in all of our lives when the wind blows cold and we feel fragile and exposed. These are the times when we wrap each other up in a blanket of love and friendship and stay right there until the buds begin to show again.

Real friendship grows when we are prepared to be there equally in the bad moments and the good. When we can walk through a field with a few thorns in the grass and make it to the other side, our friendships will be stronger and our joy will be real. We were formed for relationship, but we are filled in Christ. Our deepest needs for intimacy will be met only in the "friend who sticks closer than a brother" (Proverbs 18:24). The One who has surely carried our sorrows. The One who has known us since before we were born.

Sheila Walsh

I have only a few close friends. We're not talking casual acquaintances here. We're talking people who know me inside out—people I could trade pantyhose with, people I can trust with my darkest secret, my most delicate china, and my wildest dream. People for whom I don't have to put on makeup or straighten the house.

Only low-maintenance friends qualify for the short list! I can cut short a telephone conversation without explanation; I can NOT invite them to a dinner party, and they know I must have a good reason. They never demand more than I can give and are willing to let me sacrifice for them when they are in need. The give-and-take is joyful and genuine. (I know lots of folks who are exceptionally generous givers but so self-sufficient that they would die before they let a friend return a favor. A good friend is also a gracious receiver!)

Who are your close friends? Have you told them lately how much you appreciate them?

Joy MacKenzie

Promises About Friendship

Rejoice with those who rejoice; mourn with those who mourn.
Romans 12:15

Her neighbors and relatives heard that the LORD had shown her great mercy, and they shared her joy.
Luke 1:58

Suppose a woman has ten silver coins and loses one. Does she not light a lamp, sweep the house and search carefully until she finds it? And when she finds it, she calls her friends and neighbors together and says, "Rejoice with me; I have found my lost coin."
Luke 15:8–9

Be glad and rejoice with me.
Philippians 2:18

The Joy of a Good Attitude

My bus driver's name on this particular spring tour was "Shooter." He was kindhearted, upbeat, and very unassuming.

One day on the road, in dire need of toiletries, I was waiting in the lobby for a cab to take me to the nearest drugstore. Shooter also happened to be there.

Out of the blue, he said to me, "Kathy, you get up in the morning with a good attitude. I like that."

Nowhere near every morning, I thought. But I was thankful for his observation.

"This is how I look at it," he said. "The sun comes up every morning, and I'm grateful for another day to be alive. And you know what? If the sun never came up, we could all use a flashlight."

Shooter's words touched me deeply that day. I am a believer in Jesus and his promises. If the sun doesn't shine, I do indeed have a flashlight: His Word is a lamp unto my feet, guiding my every step. The sweet glow of his presence shines into my darkness.

Kathy Troccoli

We live out the kingdom of God within us when we treasure each other and when we find ways to turn unfortunate things around. Laughter is one of those ways. Laughter stirs the blood, expands the chest, electrifies the nerves, and clears the cobwebs from the brain. If you laugh a lot, when you are older all your wrinkles will be in the right places!

If you live to be one hundred, your heart will have beaten 3,681,619,200 times, pumping 27,323,260 gallons of blood weighing over one hundred tons. (If you end up tired, you've earned it!) Think about making every heartbeat a happy one.

Barbara Johnson

Promises About a Good Attitude

"Well done, good and faithful servant! You have been faithful with a few things; I will put you in charge of many things. Come and share your master's happiness!"
Matthew 25:21

A happy heart makes the face cheerful,
but heartache crushes the spirit.
Proverbs 15:13

Just as the sufferings of Christ flow over into our lives, so also through Christ our comfort overflows.
2 Corinthians 1:5

Rejoice that you participate in the sufferings of Christ, so that you may be overjoyed when his glory is revealed.
1 Peter 4:13

The Joy of a Loving Letter

Bill and I travel to speaking engagements as many as thirty-nine weekends a year, and sometimes we find ourselves standing in the carport on Sunday afternoons almost too exhausted to unload the luggage.

But as soon as I walk in the door, one of the first things that catches my eye is the huge stack of mail a neighbor has collected for us and left on the kitchen table.

Standing there reading the mail, my batteries are quickly recharged with joy, and pretty soon I'm scurrying around our home with a smile on my face and a song in my heart.

After the complicated work of writing another book or an exhausting trip for an extended speaking engagement, I sometimes feel as if I've given all that I can. But the joyful letters give me the strength. Who do you know who could use an uplifting word today?

Barbara Johnson

I remember the day I picked up a card that showed Winnie the Pooh and Piglet on the front walking hand in hand. Their conversation went like this:

"Pooh?" Piglet said.

"Yes, Piglet."

"Oh, nothing," Piglet said. "I just wanted to be sure of you."

I stared at it awhile, smiled, and then read it a few more times. I've asked this question of close friends at many different times in my life, in many different ways. I need the safety, the reassurance, the knowing they are right there and that I am loved.

Writing our feelings down and sending them to our loved ones is always worth the time and energy. It's amazing what often transpires. Cold walls melt, hard days take an easier turn, and bitterness gives way to forgiveness.

The saying that life is far too short and unpredictable is absolutely true. I try not to let a day go by without saying what needs to be said—or even what needs to be said again.

Kathy Troccoli

Promises About Loving Letters

How beautiful on the mountains
    are the feet of those who bring good
        news,
who proclaim peace,
    who bring good tidings,
    who proclaim salvation,
who say to Zion,
    "Your God reigns!"
                    Isaiah 52:7

A word aptly spoken
    is like apples of gold in settings of silver.
                    Proverbs 25:11

The Sovereign LORD has given
        me an instructed tongue,
to know the word that
        sustains the weary.
                    Isaiah 50:4

How good is a timely
        word!
                    Proverbs 15:23

Celebrate Joy!

Every good life is a balance of duty and bliss. We will be called upon to do things we would rather not. We have to weigh decisions by mind and spirit and by the Word of God. So make each year count. Instead of clutching it fast, give it away. "Cast your bread upon the waters" (Ecclesiastes 11:1), and it comes back pretzels!

Do you have a gift for making people laugh? Writing a short story? Baking a great loaf of bread? Do you listen well? Throw a mean softball? Can you organize anything with flair? Are you good at making money? Selling just about anything? Running a race? Put yourself in the center ring. Offer your energy to life and do it heartily, unto the LORD.

Don't forget to celebrate anything you can think of. Do things that make you aware of how great it is to be alive. Every day is worth a party, not just the cookie-cutter moments. Special occasions are everywhere. Don't always be practical and expedient. God gave us license to be outrageously happy, friendly, and rejoicing.

Barbara Johnson

We Christians might look a bit more redeemed if we learned more about partying well—finding ways to celebrate the victories and milestones in each other's lives and also celebrating the traditional (and maybe some untraditional) seasonal holidays and holy days.

Families can celebrate their own events: anniversaries, Mother's Day, Father's Day. Celebrate! I know, putting on a party, even an informal gathering, takes effort, from organizing to cleanup. But I think our society, even our church, is hungry for meaningful interaction. Forget the virtual Internet party. Have a real one that includes smiles, laughter, and popcorn. Let people gather around the grill. Skewer their own shish kebabs. Make their own pizzas. Decorate their own Christmas cookies.

Why not share the goodness of God in your life with others? Gather to celebrate because we are made for community. Sign on, sign up for the party. Celebrate the moment. Set up a milestone. Treasure the memory. Share the joy.

Sheila Walsh

Promises About Celebrations

*Let all who take refuge in you be
        glad;
    let them ever sing for joy.
Spread your protection over them,
    that those who love your name
        may rejoice in you.
For surely, O LORD, you bless the
        righteous;
    you surround them with your
        favor as with a shield.*
            Psalm 5:11–12

*One generation will commend
        your works to another;
    they will tell of your mighty acts.
They will speak of the glorious
        splendor of your majesty,
    and I will meditate on your wonderful
        works.
They will tell of the power of
        your awesome works,
    and I will proclaim your great deeds.
They will celebrate your abundant goodness
    and joyfully sing of your righteousness.*
            Psalm 145:4–7

The Joy of Family

Recently my cousin Ann, whom I had not heard from since we were children, contacted me. What a surprise, and how tickled I was to learn she wanted to reconnect after all these years. (We were raised in different states, and our life journeys never had occasion to intersect.) Ann said she woke up one day and realized she had lost contact with her father's (my uncle's) family. Now in her sixties, she decided to call all of her first cousins and reestablish relationships. I couldn't have been more pleased, and so we agreed to meet up at one of my conferences in the South. Our reunion was fun and allowed us to reestablish our family connection. Isn't that what connection is really all about—being like family?

Patsy Clairmont

Since Thanksgiving was only a few days away, I hurried off to buy a frozen turkey. I quickly grabbed a sixteen-pound Jenny O.

The directions on Jenny's frozen back instructed me to place her in my refrigerator where she would thaw. With innocent anticipation, I pulled Jenny out of the refrigerator Thanksgiving morning. She wasn't as stiff as the day we had met, but she certainly wasn't soft and pliable.

Jenny crawled into my oven around eleven o'clock and came out around five in the evening. She was flavorful and moist until I cut more than an inch deep. Then we hit pink meat, which threw me into fits about salmonella potential.

In spite of this mild turkey crisis, my family, some dear friends, and I had a wonderful time together. Sometimes I forget and allow myself to focus on the externals of a celebration, which, of course, throttles my internal experience of joy. Even if we had been reduced to ordering out for pizza and having Jenny join us in eating the meal, we would have had a great time simply because we were together.

Marilyn Meberg

Promises About Family

You are no longer foreigners and aliens,
but fellow citizens with God's people and
members of God's household.
Ephesians 2:19

Keep your father's commands
and do not forsake your mother's
teaching.
Bind them upon your heart forever;
fasten them around your neck.
When you walk, they will guide you;
when you sleep, they will watch over
you;
when you awake, they will speak to
you.
Proverbs 6:20–22

As for me and my household, we will
serve the Lord.
Joshua 24:15

Live in harmony with one another;
be sympathetic, love as brothers, be
compassionate and humble.
1 Peter 3:8

The Days of Your Life

There are days when I start feeling blue. On those days I've learned to avoid certain things. I won't weigh myself, listen to sad music, get a haircut, open a box of chocolates, or shop for a bathing suit. Instead, on such days I make it a goal to perk up and be happy. The best way is to become a joy germ carrier. Infecting people with joy so they break out in symptoms of laughter—that's the very best way to beat the blues.

I've made it a habit to wring out of every single day all the fun and love I can find. If you don't know where to start next time you're feeling low, take it simply: Fill in the hours with crazy excursions into comedy. You'll learn what makes people laugh and how to communicate through chuckles. The point is simply to get started. The point is never to give up. The point is to be friendly and to focus on the person next to you. People who like people are people that people like!

Barbara Johnson

I like having special days, days set aside to commemorate an event: birthdays, anniversaries, graduations. My journals are full of remembrances like, "Forty years ago today my parents were married." Or, "If my father had lived, he'd be ninety today." Or, "Remember, Luci, three years ago you bought this house."

Days are important. I anticipate them. I'm looking forward to the day my friends come for Thanksgiving, to the next time I'll see my brother in Florida. And I can never quite wait for Christmas.

The word *days* appears more than five hundred times in Scripture, and the Mosaic Law prescribed feast days when the congregation was to celebrate by dancing, singing, resting from labor, and giving praise to God. These were occasions of joy and gladness.

I encourage you to create special days for yourself and your family. Twenty-four hours when you do something entirely different from other days ... or maybe do nothing at all.

This is the day the LORD has made. Rejoice. Celebrate all your days.

Luci Swindoll

Promises About Your Days

This is the day the LORD has made;
let us rejoice and be glad in it.
Psalm 118:24

This day is sacred to our LORD. Do not grieve,
for the joy of the LORD is your strength.
Nehemiah 8:10

If you call the Sabbath a delight
    and the LORD's holy day honorable,
and if you honor it by not going your own
    way
    and not doing as you please or
        speaking idle words,
then you will find your joy in the LORD.
Isaiah 58:13–14

I tell you, now is the time of God's
favor, now is the day of salvation.
2 Corinthians 6:2

Renew Your Hope with Prayer

One of the most colorful people in my family is Uncle Lawrence Morris, Jr., my mother's only brother. His nickname is Uncle Brother. Although he had accepted Christ as a young man, Uncle Brother had lived like the devil. But I prayed for him to return to the LORD. I didn't want Uncle Brother to die without realizing he could enjoy a better life than the one he had chosen.

Thanks be to God, for the past several years, Uncle Brother has made some major changes. He reads his Bible. He bridles his tongue. He has changed his friends. He is concerned about others.

God was always present. And he was waiting for my uncle to reopen his heart.

Are you dealing with someone whom you feel will never change? Nobody is so far from God that he can't get back to the LORD. Our responsibility is to keep knocking at God's door about that person, to keep believing God will answer our prayers. Thank God for what he will do. Patiently but expectantly wait on the LORD. Renew your hope!

Thelma Wells

The promise to pray for someone going through hard times rolls easily off our tongues. But do we really mean it? Our sisters, brothers, and children in the faith need our committed involvement in their lives.

Prayer is not a last resort but a first-rate privilege. We don't know how to pray as we ought, but we ought to pray anyway. We never know why some things happen as they do. But we stand upon the rocky shores of life and keep on praying, because prayer changes the one who prays as much as it changes those for whom we pray.

Some people think their prayers have fallen on deaf ears. But they have not. It takes faith to know that. Faith is the ability to let your light shine even after your fuse is blown. Faith is seeing light with the eyes of your heart, when the eyes of your body see only darkness ahead.

God is changing things through our willingness to pray and keep at it. While sorrow looks back and worry looks around, faith looks up. As we pray, we may face finite disappointment, but we must never lose infinite hope.

Barbara Johnson

Promises About Renewing Your Hope

Be strong and take heart,
all you who hope in the LORD.
Psalm 31:24

The LORD longs to be gracious to you;
he rises to show you compassion.
For the LORD is a God of justice.
Blessed are all who wait for him!
Isaiah 30:18

The LORD is good to those whose
hope is in him,
to the one who seeks him;
it is good to wait quietly
for the salvation of the LORD.
Lamentations 3:25–26

Put your hope in the LORD,
for with the LORD is unfailing love
and with him is full redemption.
Psalm 130:7

Focus on Christ & Find Joy

There's really no easy formula for appropriating joy. Joy happens in us as God restores us, teaching us to abide in him as he works in and through us.

Joy is not something that you can buy. You can't get it from a book or a conference. You can't absorb it as if by osmosis by hanging out with people who seem to have it. You can spend your life trying to eliminate all pain and stress from your world in the vain hope that joy will take its place, but it won't. You can beg for it, pray for it, bargain for it, to no avail. Joy comes only when you live in relationship with the Source of joy.

Remember Jesus' promise in John 15:4? "Remain in me, and I will remain in you. No branch can bear fruit by itself; it must remain in the vine. Neither can you bear fruit unless you remain in me." You can't go out and work on joy. We are called to rest in the One who is joy. Without him there is no fruit, no joy.

Sheila Walsh

In this instant world, we often want microwave solutions to crockpot problems. I'm not ashamed to admit that I lack solutions to overwhelming troubles. Some things belong to the LORD; he alone knows these secrets. On this earth we seek advice from experts, wisdom from counselors, solace from comforters, encouragement from mentors. But when you get right down to it, the bottom line is that we must trust the LORD through it all.

Jesus is there when nobody else is. When one of God's kids hits rock bottom, he or she discovers that Jesus is the only foundation. You are not just a number in a network in cyberspace. There is Someone who knows your face, your name, your need. That person doesn't punch in a formula on a PC to arrive at a solution to your trouble. He never offers platitudes, and he never patronizes. Instead he offers love and a place to land. He gives the quiet assurance that he is all you need at any point in life.

Take a chance. Embrace the vision God gives you. Celebrate life.

Barbara Johnson

Promises About Focusing on Christ

Christ Jesus, who died—more than that, who was raised to life—is at the right hand of God and is also interceding for us.
Romans 8:34

He who began a good work in you will carry it on to completion until the day of Christ Jesus.
Philippians 1:6

Since, then, you have been raised with Christ, set your hearts on things above, where Christ is seated at the right hand of God.
Colossians 3:1

Consider him who endured such opposition from sinful men, so that you will not grow weary and lose heart.
Hebrews 12:3

The Joy of Helping Others Help You

One of the most rewarding ways to relate to others is to give them ownership over what's going on. At home the entire family should share in keeping things up around the house. At work people want to be a part of things and to have responsibility with accountability. And others in your life are waiting for you to take some items off your calendar so they can put them on theirs.

It takes awhile to complete the delegation process. Training, explaining, and overseeing are all part of it. However, when everyone has his or her tasks and can do them with little supervision, you begin to reap results.

I hypothesize that you have some people to whom you can delegate housework, office work, and church work. Wouldn't it be great not to have the frightening words, *Fire! Another fire!* reverberating in your mind? You have to decide you're tired of fighting these blazes yourself. Trust people enough to give them important tasks. Delegate.

Thelma Wells

Recently I moved. I moved only seven blocks, but I still had to pick up everything and find a place to set it down in my new abode—that or have an enormous (thirty-four years' worth of stuff) yard sale. Thankfully, I had dear friends come to my rescue and help me pack.

After arriving in my new home, I was overwhelmed at the prospect of settling in. I had thought I would pull it together rapidly. Instead, I roamed from room to room trying to remember my name. Carol came to give support (and to verify my identity) every morning for four days. She assisted me until early evening, when she would then make our dinner, serve us, and clean up. You can only guess what a gift that was to me emotionally. I never expected that kind of beyond-the-call-of-duty effort, but I'm certain that new home ownership would have found me sinking before I could even unload the cargo, if it were not for Carol's life preserver of kindness.

Patsy Clairmont

Promises About Helping Others Help Us

Moses' father-in-law said: "The work is too heavy for you; you cannot handle it alone. Listen now to me and I will give you some advice, and may God be with you. You must be the people's representative before God and bring their disputes to him. Teach them the decrees and laws, and show them the way to live and the duties they are to perform. But select capable men from all the people—men who fear God, trustworthy men who hate dishonest gain—and appoint them as officials over thousands, hundreds, fifties and tens. Have them serve as judges for the people at all times, but have them bring every difficult case to you; the simple cases they can decide themselves. That will make your load lighter, because they will share it with you. If you do this and God so commands, you will be able to stand the strain, and all these people will go home satisfied."

Exodus 18:17–23

Blessed Sidekicks

We need each other. Scripture says two are better than one. We're instructed to love, pray for, care about, accept, forgive, serve, encourage, and build up one another.

I love that about my partners in the Women of Faith conferences. We "be-bop" all over the country watching out for each other. We serve one another joyfully, from the heart. When one of us is down, we rally to her. When one celebrates, we rejoice together. We're a team. We never anticipated this kind of bonding, but bonded we are.

People need each other—no matter how much we insist we don't. Nobody is an island, an entity unto herself, or a Lone Ranger. We're in this thing called community, and part of the joy of community is sharing the weight. The weight of burdens, losses, loneliness, and fear.

Look around you, my friend. Who's there for you? And who are you there for? Take a careful look. Even those who insist they can make it on their own may be waiting for you to reach out and help. Be there and available. Even the Lone Ranger had a sidekick.

Luci Swindoll

The key to friendship between women—and somehow for us girls, it's not the easiest thing to achieve—is being able to accept each other unconditionally. If we can do that, the rewards are never ending! And the pay dirt is definitely a bonanza! It's a proven fact we will stay young longer, are less likely to be depressed, and will save a fortune in counseling fees!

The secret of friendship is that we bless each other, and within the blessing is a kaleidoscope of meaning—to make happy, to praise, to thank, to protect, to sanctify, to favor, to celebrate, to give benediction. It not only applies to best friends, but it applies to every cherished human relationship—husband and wife, parent and child, sister and brother, neighbor with neighbor, church member with church member. It's cross-cultural, cross-racial, cross-generational, and cross-backyardfence-ational—a made-up word, but that, too, is allowed with friends!

Sue Buchanan

Promises About Blessed
Sidekicks

Carry each other's burdens, and in this way
you will fulfill the law of Christ.
Galatians 6:2

You yourselves have been taught by God to
love each other.
1 Thessalonians 4:9

Be devoted to one another in
brotherly love. Honor one another
above yourselves.
Romans 12:10

If you really keep the royal law found in
Scripture, "Love your neighbor as yourself,"
you are doing right.
James 2:8

Love one another deeply, from the heart.
1 Peter 1:22

The Joy Buster of Pride

How quickly we judge another's outward appearance. We see clothes that don't match, and we judge. We look at another's car, manners, music, posture, or facial characteristics ... judging all the while.

I'll tell you, if human perspective had been the criterion for God's judgment, the Swindolls would have been zapped long ago. Each of us, my brothers and I, live the majority of our lives in well-worn clothes that don't match. More often than not, I go to the store in my oldest sweats. I don't want to change clothes just to pick up a carton of milk, grab a hamburger, or have the car washed.

In Antoine de Saint-Exupery's book, *The Little Prince*, he states, "It is only with the heart that one can see rightly; what is essential is invisible to the eye."

"What is essential is invisible" captures what we read in Scripture. We have no right to pass judgment on another. When I don't put any judgmental demands on others, I'm happiest, because I know I'm doing what is right. When nobody puts demands on me, it frees me to be who I am.

Luci Swindoll

Uppity is a downer. We are warned about being high-minded, that is, thinking more highly of ourselves than we should. Like the time I thought I was lookin' good, only to discover my pantyhose were underfoot—or more accurately, they were streaming behind my foot as I sashayed through the middle of town.

Remember in Genesis when Joseph paraded his new coat for his brothers' viewing? They, in turn, stripped him of his colors and sold him into slavery. Yep, showing off tends to trip us up. Thinking more highly of ourselves than we ought means a downfall is probably up ahead.

I guess God knew that for Joseph to grow up, he would have to live down his need to be the center of attention. Here, though, is the amazing truth: Joseph grew to handle his down times as well as he did his up times. He became an example to many as his social position looked an awful lot like a busy elevator.

Which leads me to ask, Who is the central focus of our lives? The LORD? Or our need to be center stage? Are we willing, whether we ascend or descend, to be a shining example?

Patsy Clairmont

Promises About Overcoming Pride

*Patience is better than
pride.*
Ecclesiastes 7:8

*Pride only breeds quarrels,
but wisdom is found in those
who take advice.*
Proverbs 13:10

*When pride comes, then comes
disgrace,
but with humility comes
wisdom.*
Proverbs 11:2

*Pride goes before destruction,
a haughty spirit before a fall.*
Proverbs 16:18

Everyone who exalts himself will
be humbled, and he who humbles
himself will be exalted.
Luke 18:14

The Joy of Fellowship

I'm convinced that wherever I am, Christian fellowship is mandatory for my heart and soul. Nothing can take its place.

One day outside a church in Buenos Aires, the spirited sounds of singing and clapping met us on the sidewalk, enveloped us, and literally propelled us forward. We were surrounded by radiantly smiling Latin faces singing praises to God with utter abandon. Not only was I moved by the powerful presence of the Holy Spirit in that place, but I also realized how rejuvenated I felt to be enveloped by believers. It felt wonderful to be bathed in the oneness of these dear Christians, who hugged and kissed us with such unaffected genuineness. That sweet Sunday will live forever in my memory, as I reflect on fellowship that was unhindered by language or cultural barriers.

How about you? Are you pining for the fellowship that surpasses all others? Spend time with fellow believers, rejoicing over what you have in Jesus. Sing some songs. Laugh together. Pray for one another. Hug each other. Celebrate the blessed tie that binds you to one another in Christian love.

Marilyn Meberg

A cold day. It swirls snow, kicking up a storm. It takes something extra to stick to the job, keep your kids happy in the house, get to church, and be a good neighbor in those frosty winter months.

We experience frigid temperatures in our faith, too. There are cold days when hope dies: love walks out the door, a friend moves out of town, the job ends, the bank fails. God seems distant. Prayer fades in your throat before you barely utter a word. The Bible stares back with a blank page. You might call it spiritual frostbite. It is painful. Poisonous. Dangerous.

The church is God's spiritual stove. In its containment we pile on fuel, stir the embers, strike a match. We need each other's warmth to survive the winters of our lives. Don't be fooled by the facade of strength that some put on to protect themselves. Put a little May and June into someone's life. Don't hide behind propriety. Look both ways—who needs a hand, a word, or one of your ears for a few moments? Lending yours might mean making someone's day. Reach out and warm a heart!

Barbara Johnson

Promises About Fellowship

Honor one another above yourselves. Never be lacking in zeal, but keep your spiritual fervor, serving the LORD.... Share with God's people who are in need. Practice hospitality.... Live in harmony with one another. Do not be proud, but be willing to associate with people of low position. Do not be conceited. Do not repay anyone evil for evil. Be careful to do what is right in the eyes of everybody. If it is possible, as far as it depends on you, live at peace with everyone.

Romans 12:10–18

Jesus said, "Where two or three come together in my name, there am I with them."

Matthew 18:20

The Joy of Being Different

We rang the doorbell, and I laughed as I looked through the door's glass pane and saw four shaggy dogs running over each other to be first to the door.

As we sat in our friends' study, eventually the dogs all found their places, flopping down, exhausted from extending such an effusive welcome.

"Do you make a habit of rescuing dogs from the pound?" I asked.

"Yes, I do," Karalyn answered. "Everyone wants a perfect animal, a new one that looks great with no faults or limitations, but I've found the animals who have been all but tossed away have so much love to give."

Christ said that we shouldn't entertain those who can repay us but rather those who have nothing to give. In every church across America, there are those who come lonely and leave lonely every Sunday. Old people's homes are full of forgotten lives. What a blessing it would be to them and to us if we really saw them and included them in our lives.

Sheila Walsh

Do I have the courage to be me? I hope to be a woman who is real and compassionate and who might draw people to nestle within God's embrace.

Any one of us can do that. We may never win any great awards or be named best dressed, most beautiful, most popular, or most revered. But each of us has an arm with which to hold another person. Each of us can pull another shoulder under ours. Each of us can invite someone in need to nestle next to our heart.

We can give a pat on the back, a simple compliment, a kiss on the cheek, a thumbs-up sign. We can smile at a stranger, say hello when it's least expected, send a card of congratulations, take flowers to a sick neighbor, make a casserole for a new mother.

Let's take the things that set us apart, that make us different, that cause us to disagree, and make them an occasion to compliment each other and be thankful for each other. Let us be big enough to be smaller than our neighbor, spouse, friends, and strangers. Every day.

Barbara Johnson

Promises About Being Different

The LORD has declared this day that you are his people, his treasured possession as he promised, and that you are to keep all his commands.
Deuteronomy 26:18

I will give you a new heart and put a new spirit in you; I will remove from you your heart of stone and give you a heart of flesh. And I will put my Spirit in you and move you to follow my decrees and be careful to keep my laws.
Ezekiel 36:26–27

Know that the LORD has set apart the godly for himself.
Psalm 4:3

We are God's workmanship, created in Christ Jesus to do good works, which God prepared in advance for us to do.
Ephesians 2:10

Put on a Smiley Face

I believe in having fun, because I know that she who laughs, lasts. Whatever you do, whether it's jumping from airplanes, visiting the sick, surfing the Net, taking care of widows, or goofing off, do it well, and never lose your ability to scatter joy. Tuck some in the pocket of the stranger next to you at the grocery store. Sprinkle it on the head of an elderly lady crossing the street in front of you. Leave funny messages in your teenagers' cars or on their e-mail. Wake your spouse up with the scent of roses or honeysuckle. And never ever forget to smile.

Smiles are like two-for-one coupons. Each time you let them spread across your lips, they light up the face and heart of someone else. Sooner or later a smile will come back around to you just when you need it most. And it is something anyone—everyone—can do well. Talk about a win-win situation; move over, Stephen Covey!

Barbara Johnson

Picture this: You are asked to travel for most of the weekends of an entire year around the country with five women you've never met. You'll be speaking together, eating together, and praying together. You'll be under pressure together, and you'll share in the joys and tribulations of traveling together. That's an awful lot of togetherness with a bunch of strangers, if you ask me.

If I had known what it was going to be like to travel with these five Women of Faith, I would have ... why, I would have signed up a lot sooner. I had no idea how exciting and vibrant they were, nor what an influence they would have on my life. Through all the pain, sorrow, disappointment, aggravation, and agitation of life, these wonderful women are still funny, adventurous, and silly.

Just as they have influenced and encouraged me, you, too, can be a blessing to the people you meet today. Life has its serious moments. But being just a bit kooky may be the secret to seeing yourself and others through good times and bad. Go ahead, make someone's day—make her smile.

Thelma Wells

Promises About Smiles

A happy heart makes the face
cheerful.
Proverbs 15:13

A cheerful heart is good medicine,
but a crushed spirit dries up the bones.
Proverbs 17:22

The cheerful heart has a
continual feast.
Proverbs 15:15

Rejoice in the LORD always. I will say
it again: Rejoice!
Philippians 4:4

Sing joyfully to the LORD, you
righteous;
it is fitting for the upright
to praise him.
Psalm 33:1

The Joy of Caring for Family Members

True love demands honesty, taking risks with one another, and enduring some difficult moments because we want a real relationship.

A friend of mine recently told me he now only talks to his mother by e-mail because it makes her more bearable. I asked him if he had ever discussed with her the difficulty they had communicating. He looked at me as if I had suggested he stick his hand in a blender. "You've got to be kidding," he said. "Talk to my mother? That's like trying to bargain with a scorpion!"

Often family members behave in set patterns simply because that's what we expect them to do. It's a dance that has developed over the years between us. We need to take a fresh look. Put on a new record. Say "thank you." Send flowers. Write a note. Take a good look. Move a little closer.

Sheila Walsh

Caring is a gift you give the other person. And Christian women are good at caring. The pain that sometimes results is a value-added premium to let you know that you are alive and well, that you still have a tender heart. Sympathy is nothing other than your pain in my heart.

We cannot always head off disaster. Sometimes we discover that the light at the end of the tunnel really is the headlight of an oncoming train. Even so, I've found that the best thing to hold on to in this life is each other. When even that fails, we can be assured that God is holding on to us.

I try to take the cold water thrown upon me, heat it with enthusiasm, and use the steam to push ahead. On the long journey, I seek to love and to live in the strength of the LORD. At the end of each day, before turning down the covers, I turn all my problems over to the Holy Spirit. I'm grateful he stays up late to handle them. Then I lie down, secure in the knowledge that broken things become blessed things if I let Christ do the mending!

Barbara Johnson

Promises About Caring for Family Members

If anyone does not provide for his relatives, and especially for his immediate family, he has denied the faith and is worse than an unbeliever.
1 Timothy 5:8

Let us do good to all people, especially to those who belong to the family of believers.
Galatians 6:10

Children should not have to save up for their parents, but parents for their children.
2 Corinthians 12:14

Jesus said, "Which of you fathers, if your son asks for a fish, will give him a snake instead? Or if he asks for an egg, will give him a scorpion? If you then, though you are evil, know how to give good gifts to your children, how much more will your Father in heaven give the Holy Spirit to those who ask him!"
Luke 11:11–13

A Positive Perspective

Stress is everywhere. People stress out because they know today is the tomorrow they worried about yesterday! Dieters know what stress is. Someone said, "I've been on a diet for two weeks, and all I've lost is fourteen days." That's self-imposed stress.

What happens when you think you are winning the rat race and along come faster rats? How do you deal with the stress? The best advice for stress is this: Stress may be a given factor, but your attitude can change the way it affects you.

Stress is nothing but psychological pollution. Flush stuff like that out of your system with a positive outlook. Keep mentally limber; accept what you can't change, and don't dwell on your own or others' shortcomings. Be an imp for a day or an hour, make a neighbor laugh, play a practical joke, delight yourself with a wacky surprise.

Don't waste today's time cluttering up tomorrow's opportunities with yesterday's troubles! God has promised to turn your "hours of stressing into showers of blessing."

Barbara Johnson

I love grocery shopping. I love having all those choices and anticipating the preparation of wonderful meals. I grab up fresh bouquets of flowers and never quite seem to get the smile off my face. Every now and then, I add a jar of pickles, can of hair spray, or package of liverwurst to another shopper's unattended cart, just to entertain myself and give that person whiplash at the checkout counter.

Even the post office can be rewarding. Last week, I bought ten stamps and gave two each to the five people behind me. I told them I hated waiting in line and was sure they did, too, and so I was giving them a little present. My own little random act of kindness.

We all have things in life we have to do, but we can choose how we want to do them. It's up to each of us. I can tell you this, though. There's only one way to have joy ... by doing everything "as unto the LORD."

By the way, if you're the one who arrived at home with an extra jar of pickles, enjoy them. You helped bring a smile to someone today. Perspective is everything.

Luci Swindoll

Promises About a Positive Perspective

Whatever you do, work at it with all your heart, as working for the LORD, not for men.
Colossians 3:23

Serve wholeheartedly, as if you were serving the LORD, not men, because you know that the LORD will reward everyone for whatever good he does, whether he is slave or free.
Ephesians 6:7–8

The Almighty says: "See if I will not throw open the floodgates of heaven and pour out so much blessing that you will not have room enough for it."
Malachi 3:10

Wrapped in Jesus' Joy

Joy. It's a powerful force. It looks in the face of life with all its tears and tragedy, all its ups and downs, and it wraps a blanket of eternal comfort around our shoulders. It doesn't leave the scene. Joy in the midst of pain, on the faces of our friends, in the quiet moments of our days. This gift the world seeks after and sells its soul to buy—found in the arms of the One who is joy. It has no substance without his presence.

The Book of Common Prayer includes a beautiful prayer for evening that requests God's help in various circumstances: "Tend the sick, LORD Christ, give rest to the weary, bless the dying, soothe the suffering, pity the afflicted, shield the joyous; and all for your love's sake. Amen."

Did you hear it? It was in there. It's my prayer for you. I tuck it into this page with all the love of heaven: "Shield the joyous." I pray: "Wrap them up, dear LORD. Keep them safe and kind and hopeful. Speak to them in the quiet and in the noise and in all the moments of their days ... for your sake. Amen."

Sheila Walsh

Promises About Jesus' Joy

Jesus said: "Take my yoke upon you and learn from me, for I am gentle and humble in heart, and you will find rest for your souls. For my yoke is easy and my burden is light."
Matthew 11:29–30

Jesus said: "I have told you these things, so that in me you may have peace. In this world you will have trouble. But take heart! I have overcome the world."
John 16:33

May our LORD Jesus Christ himself and God our Father, who loved us and by his grace gave us eternal encouragement and good hope, encourage your hearts and strengthen you in every good deed and word.
2 Thessalonians 2:16–17

We want to hear from you. Please send your comments about this book to us in care of zreview@zondervan.com. Thank you.

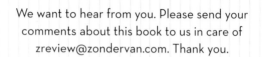